Eat Your Way Through the USA

By Loreé Pettit

Eat Your Way Through the USA
Written by Loreé Pettit

Published by Geography Matters, Inc.

Edited by Mary Jo Tate

ISBN 1-931397-34-1
Library of Congress Control Number: 2005922694
Printed in the United States of America

Dedication

I would like to dedicate *Eat Your Way Through the USA* to my grandmothers, Ophelia Stewart (Nanny) and Evelyn Ledkins (Maw). Thank you for giving me such fond childhood memories of watching and helping you in the kitchen and for passing down your love of cooking and hospitality.

Acknowledgments

To Mom, Dad, Marty, and Chalane – Thank you for patiently enduring my early trials and tribulations in the kitchen.

To my husband, Ralph – Thank you for eating the fried chicken when what you really wanted was a bologna sandwich. (Yes, there is a story behind this.)

Eat Your Way Through the USA

TABLE OF CONTENTS

Introduction

I can remember coming home from school one crisp fall afternoon when I was 8 or 9 years old and my mother greeting me at the door with a big surprise. My parents were taking us to Six Flags over Texas the next day! Now, I had been dreaming of going to Six Flags for years and was absolutely beside myself with excitement. I was so excited that I spent the whole evening trying to think of a way to thank my parents. As I finally drifted off to sleep that night, inspiration struck. Pancakes! I would make my parents from-scratch pancakes and serve them breakfast in bed before we set off on the three-hour drive to Dallas. The fact that I had never actually made pancakes didn't deter me; I'd seen Mom do it lots of times. I wasn't fazed in the least.

At 4:00 the next morning I woke up bright-eyed and bushy-tailed. Visions of my parents joyfully eating stacks of pancakes were flitting through my mind as I entered the kitchen ready to dive into my first culinary endeavor. I carefully assembled the necessary ingredients and utensils on the counter and began mixing. Keep in mind that I didn't have a recipe, so I simply put in how much I thought was needed. Never having actually worked with pancake batter before, I didn't know that it was supposed to be of a pourable consistency. Mine was more like thick dough.

Tingling with excitement and anticipating my parents' joy, I began to heat the cast-iron skillet – on high. You can imagine my father's shock and dismay when he walked into the smoke-filled kitchen to discover countertops that looked like a grenade had exploded and a platter of extremely thick "pancakes" that were burnt to a crisp on the outside and yet completely raw on the inside. Needless to say, he was less than impressed, and the dream of my parents' euphoria fell flatter than the charred pancakes. Mom was a little more understanding – after the mess was finally cleaned up – and the following Saturday cooking lessons began in earnest.

Why have I told you that story? Because children love to cook. And they enjoy working in the kitchen with their parents. Integrating food into your homeschool is an excellent opportunity to teach not only life-skills, but also to learn about foods from other places or time periods. It also gives practical, real-life application for math skills. While *Eat Your Way Through the USA* is not written as a how-to cookbook for children, I encourage you to bring the children into the kitchen with you as you prepare meals from around our great country. What a fun way to learn geography!

Recipe Selections

Researching the way our country eats was quite an adventure. Our country's eating habits are as vastly different as our terrain! I tried to choose traditional recipes that summed up each individual state as a whole, but for some states that proved to be quite a challenge. Many states have several traditional dishes, that vary by region within the state, and *Eat Your Way Through the USA* is designed to include only one meal from each state. (Some states do have bonus recipes for breakfast or snack foods.) Another element that I looked at in the selection process was whether the state was a leading producer of a certain food. As you can imagine, for several states I had to choose from among many possibilities. I hope you're not disappointed!

One dish that I purposely stayed away from was barbecue: beef versus pork; tomato, mustard, or vinegar-based sauce. So many states or cities claim to be the best that I decided to stay out of the debate.

Several of the recipes from the southern states are old family recipes that have been handed down from generation to generation, some having been written down for the first time. My husband and children certainly enjoyed the writing-down process as I had to make the dishes to figure out the measurements to write down.

One dish that I purposely stayed away from was barbecue: beef versus pork; tomato, mustard, or vinegar-based sauce. So many states or cities claim to be the best that I decided to stay out of the debate.

It is my sincerest hope that you and your family enjoy the recipes as much as I enjoyed researching and compiling them.

Bon appétit!

Alabama

Fried Catfish

1 cup flour
1 T salt
2½ cups cornmeal

2 tsp black pepper
4 lbs catfish fillets
1 cup buttermilk or evaporated milk

1. Combine flour and salt in a large shallow dish. Combine cornmeal and pepper in separate large shallow dish.
2. Dredge fillets in flour mixture. Dip in milk. Dredge in cornmeal mixture.
3. Fry in hot oil (360°) until golden. Drain on paper towels.

Baked Beans Southern Style

½ lb bacon, cooked medium well, drained, and cut into pieces (save some bacon grease)
1 medium onion, chopped
1 small green pepper, chopped

4 16-oz cans pork and beans
¼ pound ground beef, cooked
¼ cup ketchup
2 T mustard
½ cup brown sugar

1. In a medium frying pan, sauté the chopped onion and green pepper in the bacon grease until limp.
2. In a large bowl, mix the pork and beans, onions, green pepper, cut-up bacon, ground beef, ketchup, mustard, and brown sugar. Mix well until completely blended.
3. Bake, uncovered, in a 350° oven for about 1 hour; stir every 15 minutes. Turn oven down to 300°; cover and bake for at least another hour. Turn off oven and allow to sit an additional hour, covered, to get the full flavor of all the ingredients.

Peanut Butter Pie

1 envelope unflavored gelatin
½ cup boiling water
4 oz cream cheese, softened
1 cup powdered sugar
⅓ cup smooth peanut butter
8 oz non-dairy whipped topping
1 graham cracker crust

1. Dissolve gelatin in boiling water. Cool to lukewarm.
2. Whip cream cheese until soft and fluffy. Beat in sugar and peanut butter. Slowly add gelatin, blending thoroughly. Fold in whipped topping.
3. Pour into pie shell. Chill 2 hours.

FOOD FACTS

- Scientist George Washington Carver researched peanuts at the Tuskegee Institute. In all, he found over 300 uses for peanuts.
- The pecan is the official state nut.
- The turkey is the state game bird. Alabama has more wild turkeys per acre than any other state.

Crustless Salmon Quiche

4-5 oz smoked salmon, flaked
1 cup shredded Swiss cheese
1 medium onion, chopped (about ½ cup)
2 T all-purpose flour

4 eggs
1 cup milk
¾ tsp salt
⅛ tsp red pepper sauce

1. Toss salmon, cheese, and onion with the flour. Spread in greased pie pan.
2. Beat eggs slightly, then beat in remaining ingredients. Pour over salmon mixture.
3. Cook uncovered in a 350° oven 35-40 minutes or until a knife inserted in the center comes out clean. Let stand for 10 minutes before cutting.

Broccoli and Cauliflower Salad

1 T vinegar
1 T sugar
½ tsp hot sauce
1 cup mayonnaise
1 tsp salt
¾ cup sour cream
½ tsp pepper
1 bunch broccoli, chopped
1 head cauliflower, chopped
3 radishes, thinly sliced

1. Combine all ingredients except vegetables in a bowl.
2. Add vegetables.
3. Toss and chill.

Alaskan Blueberry Coffee Cake

1½ cup all-purpose flour
¾ cup sugar
2½ tsp baking powder
1 tsp salt
¼ cup vegetable oil
¾ cup milk

1 egg
1½ cup blueberries
⅓ cup all-purpose flour
½ cup brown sugar, firmly packed
½ tsp cinnamon (or more to taste)
¼ cup butter

1. In a medium mixing bowl, blend together 1½ cups flour, sugar, baking powder, salt, oil, milk, egg, and 1 cup blueberries. Beat thoroughly for 30 seconds and spread in a greased 9-inch round pan or an 8x8x2-inch pan.
2. Combine ⅓ cup flour, brown sugar, cinnamon, and butter. Sprinkle over batter and top with remaining berries.
3. Bake in a 375° oven for 25-30 minutes, until done. Don't overbake.
4. Serve warm with butter or honey.

Snow Cream

½ cup whipping cream
1 T sugar
2-3 drops vanilla
1-3 cups clean snow

1. In a separate bowl, mix cream, sugar and vanilla.
2. Slowly add snow to desired consistency.

FOOD FACTS

- Alaska is the world's largest supplier of salmon.
- Milk is Alaska's most important agricultural product.
- Alaska's growing season is short, but the long days and cool temperatures help produce fruits and vegetables that are larger than normal.
- During the Alaskan Klondike gold rush, potatoes were so valued for their vitamin C content that miners traded gold for potatoes.

Arizona

Chicken Enchiladas

2 cups cooked chicken, diced
8 oz shredded Monterey Jack cheese
1 can sliced black olives
2 tsp dried parsley
1/2 tsp garlic powder

1/2 tsp salt
1/8 tsp pepper
8 flour tortillas
1 can enchilada sauce
1/2 cup shredded cheddar cheese

1. Mix chicken, Monterey Jack, olives, and dry seasonings.
2. Divide evenly among tortillas. Roll up and place seam side down in a 9X13-inch pan.
3. Top with sauce.
4. Bake, covered, at 350° for 30 minutes.
5. Sprinkle with cheddar cheese and return to oven for 10 minutes.

Black Bean Dip

1 15-oz can black beans, drained
1 cup tomato sauce
1/2 cup shredded cheddar cheese
1 tsp chili powder
tortilla chips

1. Combine beans and tomato sauce in a saucepan; bring to a boil, stirring occasionally. Remove from heat. Cool slightly.
2. Mash bean mixture with a potato masher.
3. Add cheese and chili powder.
4. Heat, stirring constantly, until cheese melts.
5. Serve with chips.

Turtle Cheesecake

1¾ cups chocolate graham cracker crumbs
⅓ cup butter, melted
3 8-oz packages cream cheese, softened
1 14-oz can sweetened condensed milk
½ cup granulated sugar
3 large eggs
3 T lime juice

1 T vanilla
1½ cups semisweet chocolate chips
2 T chocolate syrup
2 T caramel ice cream topping
½ cup chopped pecans
¼ cup semisweet mini chocolate
  chips

1. Preheat oven to 300°.
2. Grease 9-inch springform pan.
3. Combine 1¾ cups chocolate graham cracker crumbs and butter in medium bowl. Press onto bottom and 1 inch up side of prepared pan.
4. Beat cream cheese and sweetened condensed milk in large mixing bowl until smooth. Add sugar, eggs, lime juice, and vanilla; beat until combined.
5. Microwave 1½ cups chocolate chips in medium, microwave-safe bowl on HIGH (100%) power for 1 minute; stir. If necessary, microwave at additional 10- to 15-second intervals, stirring just until chips are melted.
6. Stir 2 cups of cheesecake batter into melted chocolate; mix well.
7. Alternately spoon batters into crust, beginning and ending with yellow batter.
8. Bake for 1 hour 10 minutes or until edge is set and center moves slightly.
9. Cool in pan on wire rack for 10 minutes; run knife around edge of cheesecake. Cool completely.
10. Drizzle chocolate and caramel syrup over cheesecake. Sprinkle with pecans and mini chocolate chips.
11. Refrigerate for several hours.

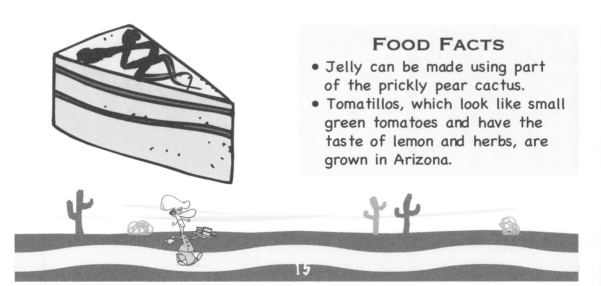

FOOD FACTS

- Jelly can be made using part of the prickly pear cactus.
- Tomatillos, which look like small green tomatoes and have the taste of lemon and herbs, are grown in Arizona.

Arkansas

Chicken and Rice

This comes from my friend Lezley.

4 boneless, skinless chicken breasts
seasoned salt
pepper
garlic powder

1 can cream of mushroom soup
1 can cream of chicken soup
milk (1 soup can full)
rice, cooked

1. Season chicken well with seasoned salt, pepper, and garlic powder. Place in baking dish.
2. In a bowl, stir soups and 1 soup can measure of milk together. Add seasoned salt and pepper, if desired. Pour over chicken.
3. Bake, covered, at 350° for 1 hour.
4. Serve with rice.

Purple Hull Peas

This is my Nanny's recipe. She made this for Sunday dinner every year when we were in town visiting.

3 cups fresh purple hull or field peas
1 T sugar
4 cups water
2 strips bacon or 2 tsp bacon drippings
1 tsp salt

1. Combine all ingredients in large cooking pot.
2. Bring to a rapid boil.
3. Turn to low and cook 40 minutes.

Arkansas Black Walnut Pound Cake

1 cup butter
½ cup shortening
3 cups granulated sugar
5 eggs
1 tsp vanilla

1 cup milk
1 tsp baking powder
3 cups flour
1 cup chopped black walnuts
powdered sugar

1. Beat butter, shortening, and sugar until light and fluffy.
2. Add eggs, 1 at a time, beating well after each addition.
3. Add vanilla to milk.
4. Add baking powder to flour.
5. Alternately add liquid and dry ingredients to batter (starting and ending with liquid).
6. Stir in walnuts.
7. Pour batter into a greased and floured bundt pan.
8. Bake at 325° for about 70 minutes or until cake tests done.
9. Dust with powdered sugar when cool.

FOOD FACTS

- Alma, Arkansas, is the spinach capital of the world.
- The pink tomato is the state fruit and the state vegetable.

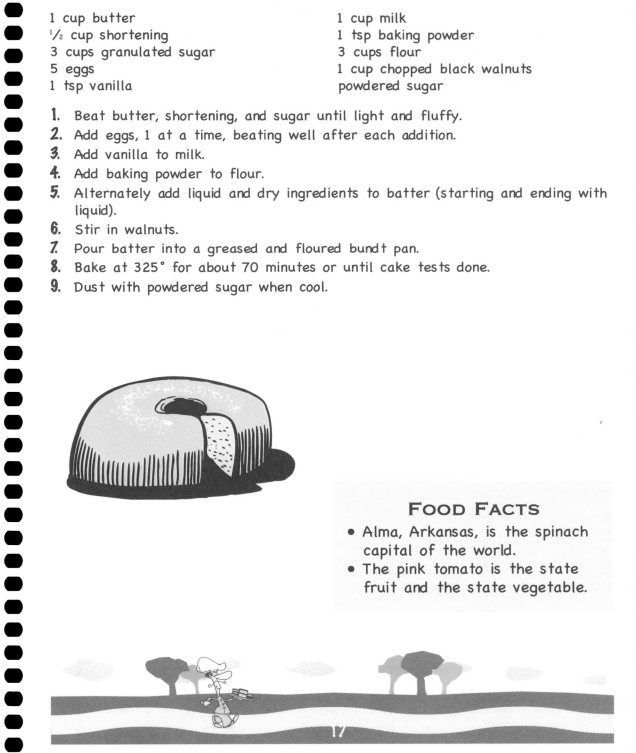

California

Cream of Broccoli Soup

Years ago when I worked in a bank, we had a new employee from California for a short time. While there, she shared with us this fabulous recipe for cream of broccoli soup. (Other vegetables can be substituted for the broccoli.)

3 cups broccoli florets, chopped
1 cup chicken broth
3 T butter
¼ cup flour

1 cup milk
1 egg, beaten
1 cup half-and-half
salt and pepper to taste

1. Cook broccoli in chicken broth 15-20 minutes.
2. Melt butter in small saucepan; add flour. Stir in milk. Cook until thick and bubbly, stirring constantly.
3. Stir butter mixture into cooked broccoli.
4. Combine eggs and half-and-half. Stir into soup.
5. Warm, but DO NOT BOIL.
6. Season and enjoy!

Seven-Layer Salad

This salad is my friend, Dari Mullin's, specialty. My husband can't get enough of it!

4 cups torn leaf lettuce
3 cups spinach
⅔ cup grated carrot
⅔ cup shredded purple cabbage
1 cup thinly sliced mushrooms

10 oz frozen peas, thawed
1 cup sour cream
1 cup mayonnaise
1 package powdered ranch dip mix
1 cup finely shredded cheddar cheese
bacon, cooked and chopped (optional)

1. Toss lettuce and spinach together in a large salad bowl; layer the next 4 ingredients.
2. Combine sour cream, mayo, and ranch dip mix in a small bowl; spread on salad.
3. Top with cheese and bacon, if desired.

California Lemon Crunch

7 oz shredded coconut
2 sticks butter, softened
½ cup firmly packed brown sugar
1½ cups uncooked oatmeal
¾ cup all-purpose flour

½ cup chopped pecans
¾ tsp ground cinnamon
½ tsp baking soda
16 oz lemon yogurt
8 oz whipped topping

1. Heat oven to 350°.
2. Place coconut in single layer in 9x13-inch baking pan. Bake 18-20 minutes or until coconut is lightly toasted, stirring after 12 minutes. Cool completely; set aside.
3. For crust, beat butter and sugar until creamy. Combine oatmeal, flour, nuts, cinnamon, and baking soda. Add to butter and sugar; mix well.
4. Reserve 1 cup coconut for topping. Stir remaining coconut into crust mixture.
5. Press dough evenly onto bottom of ungreased 9x13-inch baking pan.
6. Bake 18-20 minutes or until golden brown. Cool completely.
7. For filling, combine all remaining ingredients in large bowl. Spread mixture evenly over cooled crust.
8. Sprinkle with reserved coconut, pressing lightly.
9. Cover and refrigerate at least 3 hours.

FOOD FACTS

- California grows more lemons and broccoli than any other state.
- Fallbrook, California, is the avocado capital. More avocados are grown there than any place else in the U.S.
- California grows over 300,000 tons of grapes each year.
- Fresno, California, is the raisin capital of the world.
- California grows more than half of the fresh fruits and vegetables eaten in the United States.
- Fish tacos are popular in San Diego.

Colorado

Baked Trout with Garlic and Mushrooms

5 (¾-pound) trout
½ cup olive oil
½-¾ lb fresh mushrooms, sliced
salt and pepper
¼ cup fine dry breadcrumbs

2 T minced parsley
5 cloves garlic, minced
4 green onions, sliced
3-4 fresh lemons
¼-½ cup butter

1. Wash fish and pat dry. Coat sides with a little olive oil.
2. Place half of the mushrooms in the bottom of a shallow baking dish or cookie sheet.
3. Salt and pepper fish to taste, and place in dish on top of mushrooms.
4. Sprinkle breadcrumbs over fish along with the minced parsley, chopped garlic, and green onion. If using fresh lemons, squeeze 1 or 2 directly over the entire trout. Meanwhile melt butter and add to olive oil and the juice of 2 lemons. Pour half of mixture slowly over fish.
5. Bake for 20-25 minutes at 375° or until they are tender and breadcrumbs are light brown. Fish is done when the meat flakes easily when a fork is inserted into the flesh and lifted up slightly.
6. Just before fish are done, saute remaining mushrooms in the remaining sauce.
7. Place fish on individual plates; top evenly with sauteed mushrooms and sauce.

Potatoes Au Gratin

¼ cup butter
¼ cup all-purpose flour
2½ cups milk
2 tsp onion powder

1 tsp salt
⅛ tsp pepper
¾ cup shredded American cheese
5 large potatoes, peeled and thinly sliced

1. Melt butter in saucepan; stir in flour. Whisk in milk; stir until thick and bubbly.
2. Stir in onion powder, salt, and pepper. Stir in cheese until melted.
4. Place half of the potatoes in a 2-quart casserole dish that has been lightly coated with cooking spray. Pour half of the sauce over potatoes.
5. Repeat with remaining potatoes and sauce.
6. Bake, covered, at 350° for 45 minutes. Uncover and bake 30 more minutes.

Mile-High Strawberry Dessert

1 cup flour
¼ cup brown sugar
½ cup chopped nuts
½ cup melted butter

1. Mix all ingredients; spread evenly in 9-inch shallow baking pan.
2. Bake at 350° for 20 minutes.
3. Let cool and sprinkle ⅔ of crumb mixture in a 1-quart square dish.

2 egg whites
⅔ cup sugar
1 cup whipping cream, whipped

2 T lemon juice
2 cups sliced fresh strawberries

1. Beat egg whites until stiff peaks form, gradually adding sugar.
2. Fold in the whipped cream and remaining ingredients.
3. Spoon this over the first mixture of crumbs and smooth out.
4. Top with the remainder of the crumb mixture.
5. Freeze for 6 hours or overnight.

FOOD FACTS

- While cooking for workers on the Transcontinental Railroad, Chinese cooks invented the western omelet. They substituted peppers, onions, and ham for ingredients in Egg Fu Yung.
- Louis Ballast of Denver, Colorado, was given a trademark for the name "cheeseburger" in 1936. He never enforced it, though.

Connecticut

New England Pot Roast

¼ cup flour
1 T plus 2 tsp salt
1¼ tsp pepper
4 lbs lean boned beef chuck roast
2 T vegetable broth or butter
5 oz prepared horseradish
1 cup water
8 small potatoes, pared and halved
8 small carrots, halved crosswise
8 small onions
½ tsp salt
10¼ oz canned beef gravy (optional)

1. Stir together flour, salt, and pepper; rub mixture on meat.
2. Heat broth or butter in Dutch oven; brown meat over medium heat, about 15 minutes.
3. Reduce heat; spread horseradish on both sides of meat. Add water; cover tightly and simmer on top of range about 4 hours or until meat is tender.
4. About 1 hour BEFORE end of cooking time, add vegetables and ½ tsp salt.
5. Serve with gravy, if desired.

Crumb Cake

2 cups granulated sugar
3 cups sifted flour
1 tsp cinnamon
1 tsp cloves
½ tsp nutmeg
¼ tsp salt

1 cup butter
2 tsp baking soda
2 cups buttermilk
1 cup raisins
1 cup nuts

1. Grease and flour a 9x13-inch pan.
2. In a large bowl combine sugar, flour, spices, and salt. Work in butter until the mixture resembles coarse crumbs. Remove and reserve 1 cup of crumbs for topping.
3. Add baking soda to buttermilk and stir into remaining mixture.
4. Add raisins and nuts while there are still a few dry lumps, and continue stirring only until all is moistened.
5. Pour batter into pan; sprinkle with reserved crumbs.
6. Bake at 350° until top is browned and a toothpick comes out clean, about 50 minutes.

FOOD FACTS

- The world's first lollipop was made in New Haven, Connecticut, in 1908. It was named after a race horse, Lolly Pop.
- New Haven is also credited with creating an all-American classic-the hamburger-in 1900.
- PEZ® Candy is made in Orange, Connecticut.
- In colonial Connecticut, pumpkin halves were used as guides for haircuts.

Delaware

Peppered Beef Tip Roast

2 tsp dry mustard
½ tsp ground allspice
2 tsp cracked black pepper
1 large clove garlic, crushed

1/2 tsp ground red pepper
1 tsp vegetable oil
4-6 lbs beef round tip roast
1 cup water

1. Combine spices and oil. Rub evenly into surface of beef roast.
2. Place in baking pan. Add 1 cup water to bottom of pan.
3. Roast, covered, in 325° oven approximately 2-2½ hours for medium rare; 2½-3 hours for medium. Remove roast when thermometer registers 140° for medium rare, 155° for medium.

Broccoli-Cauliflower Casserole

1 cup water
1 large head cauliflower, broken into florets
1 medium bunch broccoli, cut into florets
¼ cup butter
¼ cup all-purpose flour
2 cups half-and-half
½ tsp salt
¼ tsp ground nutmeg
¼ tsp pepper
¼ cup shredded cheddar cheese

1. In a saucepan, bring water to a boil; add cauliflower and broccoli. Reduce heat; cover and simmer for 10-12 minutes. Drain vegetables and rinse with cold water.
2. In a saucepan, melt butter; stir in flour until smooth. Gradually add half-and-half. Bring to a boil; cook and stir for 2 minutes or until thickened. Stir in salt, nutmeg, and pepper.
3. Arrange cauliflower and broccoli in a 9x13-inch baking dish.
4. Top with cream sauce and cheese. Bake uncovered at 325° for 45 minutes.

Peach Crisp

1 cup all-purpose flour
1/2 cup sugar
1/2 cup firmly packed brown sugar
1/4 tsp salt
1/2 tsp cinnamon
1/2 cup butter
4 cups sliced peaches (fresh is best)
1 T lemon juice
2 T water

1. Combine flour, sugars, salt, and cinnamon; cut in butter with pastry blender or fork until crumbly.
2. Combine peaches, lemon juice, and water. Spoon into an 8-inch square pan.
3. Sprinkle crumb mixture over peaches.
4. Bake at 350° for 1 hour.

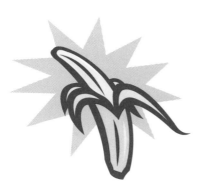

FOOD FACTS

- The sheaf of wheat, ear of corn, and the ox on the state seal symbolize the farming activities of colonial Delaware.
- More bananas enter the United States through the port in Wilmington, Delaware, than through any other seaport in the country.

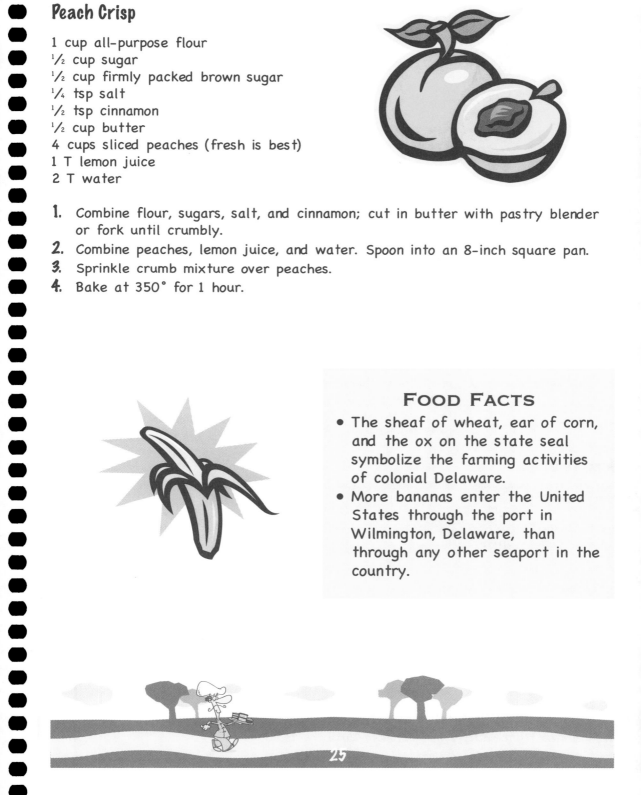

Key West Grouper

¼ cup teriyaki sauce
½ tsp grated lime peel
1 T orange juice

2 tsp lime juice
4 grouper filets

1. Combine first 4 ingredients; pour over fish in large plastic bag. Press air out of bag; close top securely. Refrigerate 45 to 60 minutes; turn bag over occasionally. Reserve marinade.
2. Cook fish on grill 4 inches from hot coals 4 minutes. Turn fish over; brush with reserved marinade. Cook 3-4 minutes longer, or until fish flakes easily with fork. Sprinkle with parsley. (OR, broil fish 4-5 inches from heat 4 minutes. Turn fish over; brush with reserved marinade. Broil 3-4 minutes longer, or until fish flakes easily with a fork.)

Tomato Grits

Yes, fish and grits go together. These two recipes are what you will find in south Florida. Those of us from northwest Florida enjoy our fish fried and our grits with cheese.

2 slices bacon
28 oz chicken broth
½ tsp salt
1 cup white corn grits

2 large tomatoes, peeled and chopped
⅛ cup chopped green chiles (optional)
1 cup cheddar cheese

1. Fry bacon; reserve drippings; crumble.
2. Pour chicken broth into a saucepan. Add salt and bacon drippings. Bring to a boil.
3. Whisk in grits with a fork to avoid lumps.
4. Stir in tomatoes and green chiles.
5. Return to a boil; reduce heat and simmer, covered, 15-20 minutes. Stir often.
6. Remove from heat; stir in cheese until melted.

Seminole Citrus Drink

1 fresh orange
1 fresh lemon
½ cup water
¼ cup sugar or honey

1. Squeeze the juice from the fruit into a large measuring cup or small bowl.
2. Add the water and sugar or honey.
3. Pour into 2 glasses filled with ice.

Key Lime Pie

4 eggs, lightly beaten
1 cup sugar
⅓ cup key lime juice

dash of salt
½ cup butter, softened
graham cracker crust
whipped cream

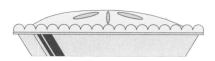

1. Combine eggs, sugar, lime juice, and salt in a double boiler.
2. Once water in bottom pot is boiling, reduce heat to low. Cook, whisking constantly, until thickened.
3. Add butter. Cook, whisking constantly, until butter melts and mixture thickens.
4. Pour into crust.
5. Bake at 300° for 20 minutes or until set.
6. Cover and chill several hours.
7. Serve with whipped cream.

FOOD FACTS

- Florida grows more limes than any other state.
- Key limes are grown in the Florida Keys. They are a unique variation of lime that is believed to have been brought to the Keys by Christopher Columbus.
- Orange juice is Florida's official state drink.
- Orange trees are not native to Florida. They were introduced by Spanish explorers around 500 years ago.

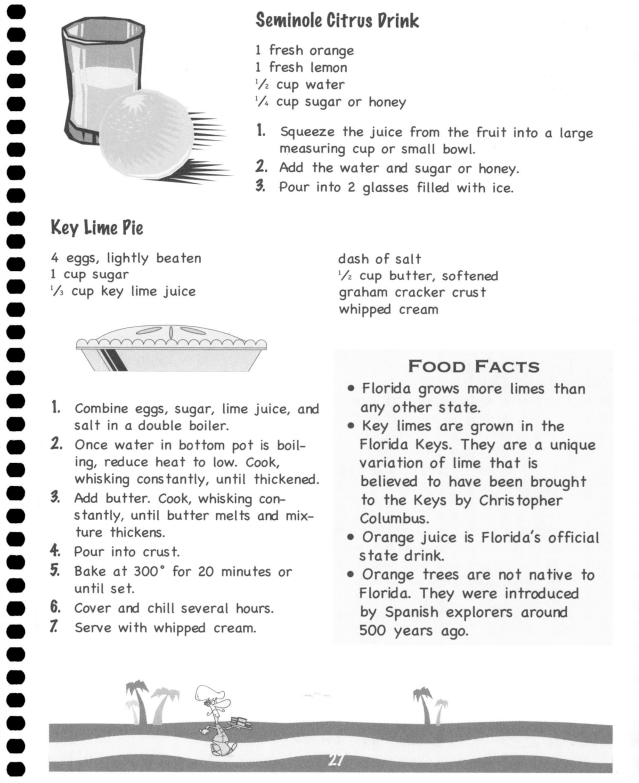

Georgia

Chicken Delight

Very popular in North Georgia

4 chicken breasts
1 can cream of mushroom soup
8 oz sour cream

$\frac{1}{2}$–$\frac{2}{3}$ cup milk
salt and pepper
1 sleeve Ritz crackers, crushed
butter, melted

1. Boil chicken. Cool and chop.
2. Combine chicken, soup, sour cream, and milk. Salt and pepper to taste.
3. Pour into shallow baking dish.
4. Top with crackers.
5. Drizzle with butter.
6. Bake at 350° until bubbly and crackers are golden.

Coca-Cola Salad

One of my sister's childhood favorites

1 can pitted Bing cherries
1 20-oz can crushed pineapple in juice
1 3-oz box black cherry gelatin (Jell-O)
1 3-oz box strawberry gelatin (Jell-O)
12 oz Coca-Cola, chilled
8 oz cream cheese, crumbled
1 cup chopped pecans

1. Drain fruit, reserving liquid.
2. Bring reserved juice to a boil.
3. Add gelatin; stir until dissolved.
4. Cool slightly and add Coca-Cola. Cool a little while longer.
5. Add cream cheese and pecans.
6. Chill until firm.

28

Boiled Peanuts

A staple in the South

1½ lbs green or raw peanuts in their shells
¾ cup salt
16 cups water

1. Rinse any dirt and debris off peanuts.
2. Combine peanuts, water, and salt in a large stockpot. Bring to a boil.
3. Reduce heat, cover, and simmer for 10 hours. Add water if needed throughout cooking time.
4. May be eaten hot or cold.

Peach Pie

5½ cups sliced fresh peaches
1 cup sugar
½ tsp cinnamon
¼ cup all-purpose flour

3 T butter
1 tsp vanilla
2 pie crusts

1. Combine peaches, sugar, cinnamon, and flour in a saucepan; set aside until syrup forms. Bring to boil; reduce heat and cook 10 minutes.
2. Remove from heat and stir in butter and vanilla. Pour into bottom pie crust.
3. Top with remaining pie crust. Fold and crimp edges. Cut slits in top crust. Loosely tent edges with foil to prevent overbrowning.
4. Bake at 425° for 15 minutes. Reduce heat to 350° and bake 30 more minutes.

FOOD FACTS

- Georgia is the leading grower of peanuts, its official state crop.
- Coca-Cola was invented at a drugstore in Cartersville, Georgia.
- The peach is Georgia's official state fruit.
- In 1990, Georgia made the Vidalia onion the official state vegetable.
- In 2002, Georgia designated grits as the official state prepared food.
- Cordele, Georgia, is the watermelon capital of the world.
- Atlanta, Georgia, is home to the Varsity, the world's largest drive-in restaurant.

Hawaiian Chicken

An advantage of growing up in a military family is that you meet people from all over the world and share recipes. This family favorite came to us from a neighbor from Hawaii while we were stationed in Texas.

1 chicken, cut up and skinned,
   or 6 chicken breasts, skinned
salt
pepper
paprika
garlic powder

1 cup flour
$\frac{1}{2}$ cup oil
1 46-oz can pineapple juice
$\frac{1}{3}$ cup soy sauce
1 $8\frac{1}{2}$-oz can crushed pineapple
1 $6\frac{1}{2}$-oz can mushrooms, drained

1. Season chicken with salt, pepper, paprika, and garlic powder.
2. Coat chicken with flour and brown in oil. Remove from pan and set aside.
3. Add 1-2 T flour to oil to make roux. To roux, add $\frac{3}{4}$ can pineapple juice and soy sauce. Bring to a boil.
4. Return chicken to pan and add crushed pineapple and mushrooms.
5. Reduce heat and simmer for 1 hour.
6. Serve with rice.

Spinach Salad

2 to 3 lbs fresh baby spinach
3 T soy sauce
3 T sesame oil

3 T vinegar
1 clove garlic, minced
$\frac{1}{2}$ T sugar or honey
3 T sesame seeds, toasted

1. Remove stems from spinach, tear larger leaves, and place in large salad bowl.
2. Combine remaining ingredients except sesame seeds.
3. Just before serving, toss spinach with dressing and sprinkle with sesame seeds.

Coconut Cake

18¼ oz white or yellow cake mix
8 oz sour cream
8½-oz can cream of coconut

¼ cup oil
3 eggs
2 cups unsweetened coconut

1. Blend first 5 ingredients with an electric mixer on low for 1 minute; scrape down sides of bowl. Beat 2 more minutes on medium speed.
2. Pour into a 9x13-inch pan that has been coated with cooking spray.
3. Bake at 350° for 40-42 minutes. Cool 20 minutes.
4. Toast 2 cups unsweetened coconut while cake cools.
5. Frost cake and top with toasted coconut.

Frosting:

8 oz cream cheese, softened
2 T milk
3¾ cup powdered sugar
1 tsp vanilla

1. Beat cream cheese 30 seconds.
2. Add remaining ingredients; beat until moistened. Scrape down sides. Beat 2 more minutes on medium.

FOOD FACTS

- Hawaii is the only state that grows coffee.
- More than ⅓ of the world's commercial supply of pineapples comes from Hawaii.
- The island of Hawaii grows most of the world's macadamia nuts.
- Hawaii is the only state that grows cacao beans to produce chocolate.
- Oranges were introduced to Hawaii in 1792.
- Hawaiian feasts are called luaus.

Potato Chip Chicken

4 oz potato chips
1/4 tsp garlic salt

black pepper, to taste
2 1/2-3 lbs chicken, cut up
1/2 cup butter, melted

1. Crush potato chips and mix with garlic salt and black pepper.
2. Dip chicken in butter, then roll in potato chips. Place on cookie sheet. Top with any remaining potato chips.
3. Bake at 375° for 1 hour.

Cottage Potato Pie

6 medium potatoes
2 cups cottage cheese
1/2 cup sour cream
1/2 tsp salt
1/4-1/2 tsp black pepper
2 T Dijon mustard

1 unbaked pie shell
4 oz Swiss cheese
2 T butter
1/2 cup Parmesan cheese
tomato slices

1. Peel, slice, and boil potatoes. Mash well.
2. Mix with cottage cheese, sour cream, salt, and pepper.
3. Spread mustard in pie shell.
4. Fill with half of potato mixture. Layer with Swiss cheese. Top with remaining potato mixture.
5. Dot with butter. Sprinkle with Parmesan cheese.
6. Bake at 375° for 40 minutes.
7. Arrange tomato slices in a single layer on pie. Return to oven for 10 more minutes.
8. Cool for 30-45 minutes before serving.

Potato Chip Cookies

3 cups all-purpose flour
2 cups crushed potato chips
1 cup chopped nuts

1 pound butter
2 cups sugar
1 tsp vanilla
powdered sugar

1. Mix together all ingredients except powdered sugar.
2. Bake at 325° for 15 minutes. Cool.
3. Roll in powdered sugar

FOOD FACTS

- Idaho grows more than 10 billion pounds of potatoes each year, earning the top spot among potato-growing states.
- Frozen French fries were created by Jack Simplot in the early 1950s.
- The world's largest potato chip is 25 feet long and 14 feet wide. It actually should be called a potato crisp since it was processed and formed. But whatever you call it, it is on display in Blackfoot, Idaho.
- It is against the law in Idaho to give anyone a box of candy that weighs more than 50 pounds.

Lasagna

1 lb ground beef
3 15-oz cans tomato sauce
1 T Italian seasoning
$\frac{1}{2}$ tsp garlic powder

8 oz mozzarella, shredded (reserve $\frac{1}{2}$ cup)
16 oz cottage cheese
12 lasagna noodles, cooked

1. Brown ground beef; drain.
2. Combine ground beef, tomato sauce, Italian seasoning, and garlic powder in large saucepan.
3. Bring to a boil; reduce heat to low; simmer, covered, 30 minutes. Add cheeses to sauce.
4. In a 9x13-inch pan, place a layer of sauce, then a layer of noodles; repeat until pan is full.
5. Top with reserved $\frac{1}{2}$ cup mozzarella.
6. Cover and bake for 30 minutes at 350°.

Serve with tossed salad.

Zucchini Skillet

2 tbsp. butter
1 tbs. vegetable oil
2 onions, chopped
1 green pepper, chopped
1 cup canned corn

4 small zucchini, sliced
2 cups tomatoes, chopped
1 tsp dried oregano, crushed
1 tsp salt
$\frac{1}{8}$ tsp pepper

1. In a large skillet melt butter with oil.
2. Saute onion and green pepper.
3. Stir in remaining ingredients.
4. Cook on low, stirring frequently, 15-20 minutes.

Italian Cream Cake

½ cup butter, softened
½ cup shortening
2 cups sugar
5 eggs
2 cups all-purpose flour

1 tsp baking soda
1 cup buttermilk
1 tsp vanilla
1 cup pecan pieces
3½ oz flaked coconut

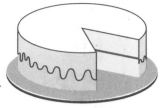

1. Cream butter, shortening, and sugar. Add eggs.
2. In a small bowl, stir together flour and baking soda.
3. Alternately beat in buttermilk and flour. Add vanilla. Stir in coconut and pecans.
5. Pour into 3 greased and floured 9-inch round pans.
6. Bake at 350° for 20-25 minutes. Cool completely before frosting.

Frosting

8 oz cream cheese
1 box powdered sugar

1 stick butter, softened
1 tsp vanilla

1. Cream butter and cream cheese.
2. Add powdered sugar and vanilla; beat until fluffy.

FOOD FACTS

- Kraft Foods, Oscar Mayer, and Louis Rich were all started in Illinois.
- Illinois is the world's leading producer of horseradish.
- Illinois is the largest producer of pumpkin in the country.
- Twinkies snack cakes were invented in 1930 by James Dewar of the Continental Baking Company in Chicago.
- The first Dairy Queen opened in 1940 in Joliet, Illinois.
- The first deep-dish pizza was created in Chicago in 1943.
- In 1961, McDonald's fast food restaurant opened its training school, Hamburger University, in Oak Brook, Illinois.
- In 1995, Nabisco produced 16 billion Oreo cookies at its Chicago factory, the largest of its kind in the world.

These recipes came from my friend, Geri, a native Hoosier.

Hot Dog Casserole

1 16-oz can pork and beans
1 package plump hot dogs, cut in half lengthwise
10 oz canned chili sauce
hot sauce, to taste
1 cup shredded cheddar cheese

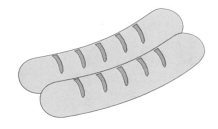

1. Pour beans into 9x13-inch casserole dish.
2. Arrange hot dog halves in a single layer on top of beans. Pour chili evenly over hot dogs.
3. Sprinkle with hot sauce. Top with cheese.
4. Bake at 350° for 15-20 minutes.

Corn Pudding

3 T plain flour
¾ tsp salt
1 T sugar
¾ cup milk

3 T butter
1 17-oz can cream corn
3 eggs, beaten

1. Mix flour, salt, and sugar together in a small bowl; set aside.
2. In a saucepan, bring milk and butter to a boil, then remove from heat. Whisk in flour mixture.
3. Stir in cream corn. Add eggs and mix well.
4. Pour into baking dish and bake at 325° until set in center.

Indiana Sugar Pie

4 T all-purpose flour
2 T cold butter
1 cup sugar
pinch of salt
single pie crust

1 cup heavy whipping cream
1 cup milk
1 tsp vanilla
ground nutmeg, for garnish

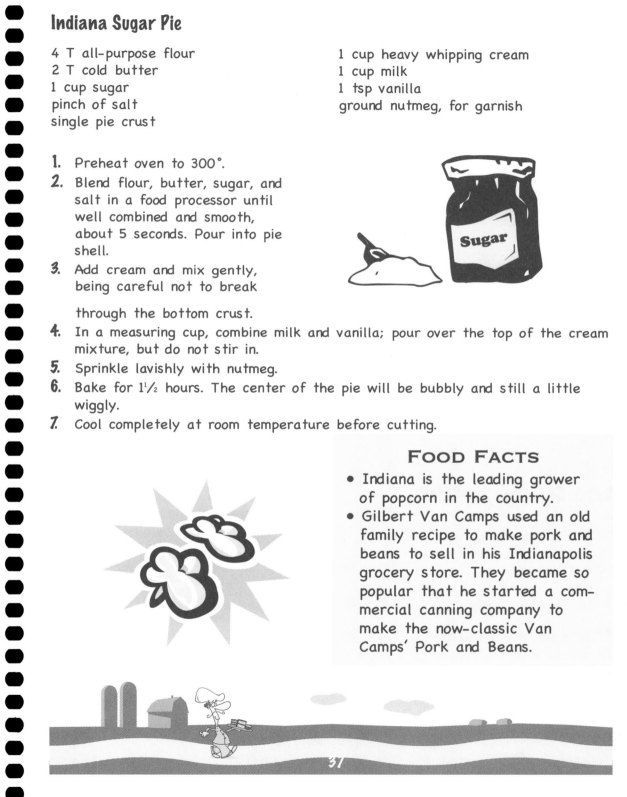

1. Preheat oven to 300°.
2. Blend flour, butter, sugar, and salt in a food processor until well combined and smooth, about 5 seconds. Pour into pie shell.
3. Add cream and mix gently, being careful not to break through the bottom crust.
4. In a measuring cup, combine milk and vanilla; pour over the top of the cream mixture, but do not stir in.
5. Sprinkle lavishly with nutmeg.
6. Bake for 1½ hours. The center of the pie will be bubbly and still a little wiggly.
7. Cool completely at room temperature before cutting.

FOOD FACTS

- Indiana is the leading grower of popcorn in the country.
- Gilbert Van Camps used an old family recipe to make pork and beans to sell in his Indianapolis grocery store. They became so popular that he started a commercial canning company to make the now-classic Van Camps' Pork and Beans.

Pork Chops and Gravy

½ cup plain flour
½ tsp salt
1½ tsp dry mustard

½ tsp garlic powder
6 lean pork chops
2 10¾-oz cans condensed chicken broth

1. Combine flour, salt, dry mustard, and garlic powder in a shallow dish.
2. Dredge chops in flour mixture and set aside.
3. Whisk remaining flour mixture into undiluted chicken broth in Crock-Pot.
4. Brown chops in hot oil and place in Crock-Pot.
5. Cook on high 2-2½ hours or until tender. Serve with rice.

Green Bean and Pea Salad

This recipe came from my husband's family, who are natives of Mt. Sterling, Iowa.

16-oz can French-cut green beans
16-oz can English peas
½ cup vinegar
1 onion, chopped
2 cups chopped celery

¼ cup pimiento, chopped
1 bell pepper, chopped
¾ cup sugar
¼ cup oil
salt and pepper to taste

1. Drain beans and peas.
2. Combine all ingredients.
3. Refrigerate at least 8 hours before serving.

Iowa Brownies

½ cup butter
1 cup sugar
1 16-oz can chocolate syrup

4 eggs
1 cup all-purpose flour
1 cup chopped nuts

1. Cream butter and sugar till fluffy.
2. Beat in syrup, then add eggs 1 at a time.
3. Beat in flour gradually.
4. Fold in nuts.
5. Pour into greased 9x13-inch pan.
6. Bake at 350° about 30-40 minutes. Brownies will not rise much.

Icing:

1 stick butter/margarine
1½ cup sugar

⅓ cup evaporated milk
½ cup chocolate chips

1. In saucepan combine butter, sugar, and evaporated milk. Bring to boil. Boil 1 minute.
2. Stir in chocolate chips; heat and stir until melted.
3. Frost brownies RIGHT AWAY with wet knife. Frosting will be thin and glossy, but sets up on the brownies. (In hot weather, place in refrigerator for about 20 minutes to aid in "setting up.")

FOOD FACTS

- An orchard outside East Peru, Iowa, is credited with developing the Red Delicious apple.
- During the height of the growing season, Iowa's corn will actually grow up to 5 inches per day.
- Almost 90% of Iowa's land is used for farming.
- Quaker Oats, in Cedar Rapids, Iowa, is the largest cereal company in the world.

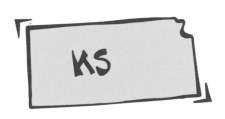

Kansas

Whole Wheat Pancakes

1⅓ cups whole wheat flour
1½ tsp baking powder
¼ tsp salt
¼ tsp baking soda

1 egg
1⅓ cups buttermilk
1 T brown sugar
1 T oil

1. In medium bowl, stir or sift first 4 ingredients together.
2. Beat egg, buttermilk, brown sugar, and oil together. Stir into dry ingredients just until moistened. Batter should be slightly lumpy.
3. Pour ¼ cup batter for each cake onto a well-seasoned hot griddle. Turn when bubbles appear on surface. Turn only once.

Oven-Fried Pork Chops

3 T butter
1 egg, beaten
2 T milk
4 pork chops
1 cup stuffing mix

1. Melt butter in a 9x13-inch pan. Whisk together egg and milk.
2. Dip pork chops into egg mixture; coat with stuffing mix. Place in 9x13-inch pan.
3. Bake at 425° for 20 minutes. Turn and bake 10-15 more minutes or until no longer pink.

Sweet Potato Soufflé

3 cups mashed sweet potatoes
¼ cup milk
1 cup sugar
½ cup butter
2 eggs
1 tsp vanilla

1. Mix all ingredients together. Pour into a buttered 2-quart baking dish.
2. Sprinkle with topping. Bake at 350° for 30 minutes. *Note: If using canned sweet potatoes, reduce sugar to ½ cup.

Topping:
1 cup brown sugar
⅓ cup butter
⅓ cup flour
1 cup chopped pecans

1. Combine dry ingredients.
2. Cut in butter until crumbly.

40

Sunflower Cookies

1¼ cup flour
1 tsp baking soda
½ tsp baking powder
1 cup butter, softened
1 cup sugar
1 cup packed brown sugar

2 eggs
1 tsp vanilla
2 cups quick oats
1 cup shredded coconut
1 cup shelled sunflower seeds

1. Combine flour, baking soda, and baking powder. Set aside.
2. Using an electric mixer, beat butter for 30 seconds. Add both sugars and beat until well mixed.
3. Add eggs and vanilla; mix well.
4. Add flour mixture and mix until combined.
5. Stir in oats, coconut, and sunflower seeds.
6. Drop dough by rounded tablespoons onto greased cookie sheets, 3 inches apart.
7. Bake at 375° for 8-9 minutes or until lightly browned.

FOOD FACTS

- Kansas is the country's leading producer of wheat and flour.
- In 1958, Pizza Hut opened its first restaurant in Wichita, Kansas.
- The oldest hamburger chain, White Castle, was founded in 1921 in Wichita, Kansas.
- In Kansas, it was once against the law to serve ice cream on cherry pie.

Hot Browns

8 thick slices bread
1 pound thinly sliced turkey breast
cheese sauce

8 slices cooked bacon
tomato slices

1. Toast bread. Top evenly with turkey.
2. Pour ½ cup cheese sauce on each sandwich.
3. Broil 6 inches from heat until bubbly and lightly browned.
4. Top with bacon and tomato slices.

Cheese sauce:

½ cup butter
⅓ cup plain flour
3½ cups milk

½ cup cheddar or Parmesan cheese
¼ tsp salt
¼ tsp pepper

1. Melt butter in saucepan. Whisk in flour.
2. Gradually whisk in milk. Bring to a boil and cook, whisking constantly, until thickened.
3. Stir in cheese until melted. Stir in salt and pepper.

Coleslaw

1 head cabbage, finely chopped
1 carrot, shredded
⅓ cup sugar
½ tsp salt
¼ tsp pepper

¼ cup milk
½ cup mayonnaise
¼ cup buttermilk
1½ T white vinegar
2½ T lemon juice

1. Combine sugar, salt, pepper, milk, mayonnaise, buttermilk, vinegar, and lemon juice and beat until smooth.
2. Add cabbage and carrots and mix well.
3. Cover and refrigerate for at least 2 hours before serving.

Kentucky Derby Pie

2 eggs, slightly beaten
1 cup sugar
½ cup margarine, melted
½ cup flour
1 tsp vanilla
¾ cup pecan halves/pieces
¾ cup chocolate chips

1. Mix ingredients in order given.
2. Pour into an unbaked 9-inch pie crust.
3. Bake at 350° for 30 minutes.

FOOD FACTS

- Colonel Harland Sanders, founder of Kentucky Fried Chicken, began cooking for hungry travelers at his service station in Corbin, Kentucky. Since this was before he had a restaurant, he served them at his own dining table in the living quarters of his service station.
- Bibb lettuce was first cultivated in Kentucky by Jack Bibb in the late 1800s.
- The Jif plant in Lexington, Kentucky, is reportedly the largest peanut butter factory in the world.
- The Hot Brown Sandwich was created at the Brown Hotel in Lexington in 1926.

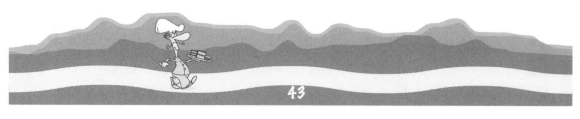

Louisiana

Cajun Gumbo

4 split chicken breasts
12 cups water
½ lb smoked or andouille sausage, sliced
1 bell pepper, chopped
1 onion, chopped
3 stalks celery, chopped

3-4 cups sliced okra
2 T oil
¼ cup flour
1 lb shrimp, peeled and deveined
salt, garlic powder, and Cajun seasoning
rice, cooked

1. Boil chicken in water for 1 hour. Remove chicken from pot and set aside to cool.
2. Heat oil in a small pan. Stir in flour. Whisk in 2 cups of chicken broth from pot. When thickened, whisk this mixture back into pot of broth.
3. Remove chicken from bone and return to pot. Add remaining ingredients, except shrimp. Simmer for 1 hour or more. Add shrimp 15 minutes before serving.
4. Serve over rice.

Natchitoches Meat Pies

2 tsp shortening
2 tsp all-purpose flour
1½ lbs ground pork
½ lb ground beef
2 large onions, chopped
6 green onions, chopped
1 T parsley

1 tsp salt
¼ tsp sage
⅛ tsp garlic powder
⅛ tsp pepper
⅛ tsp ground red pepper
1-2 packages Unroll and Bake pie crust
oil

1. Combine shortening and flour in a large Dutch oven. Cook over medium heat, stirring constantly, until roux is the color of a copper penny.
2. Add meats, onions, and seasonings. Cook until meat is browned and onions are tender. Drain well and cool.
3. Cut 22 5-inch circles from pie crust.
4. Place about 2 T of meat mixture into the center of each circle and fold in half. Moisten edges with water and press with a fork to seal.
5. Heat 1 inch of oil to 375°. Fry pies in hot oil until golden, turning once. Drain on paper towels.

Praline Cheesecake

³/₄ cup brown sugar
³/₄ cup sugar
³/₄ cup half-and-half

3 T butter
1¼ cup pecans
½ tsp vanilla

1. Butter the bottom of heavy saucepan. Cook brown sugar, sugar, half-and-half, and butter over low heat until sugars dissolve and butter melts. Stir in pecans.
2. Bring to a boil over medium heat, stir constantly 6-8 minutes or until candy thermometer reads 238°. Remove from heat.
3. Stir in vanilla and let stand 3 minutes. Beat with wooden spoon 3 minutes. Drop by tablespoonfuls onto waxed paper. Cool completely.

Icing:

2 cups pecan shortbread cookies, crushed
3 T butter, melted
4 pralines, crumbled
5 8-oz packages cream cheese
1³/₄ cups sugar
2 T plain flour
½ T vanilla

4 eggs
2 egg yolks
⅓ cup whipping cream
1 tsp lemon juice
16 oz sour cream
⅓ cup sugar

1. Combine cookie crumbs and butter. Press into bottom and sides of greased 10-inch springform pan. Bake at 350° for 8 minutes. Cool. Sprinkle praline crumbles over crust.
2. Beat cream cheese with electric mixer until creamy. Gradually add 1³/₄ sugar, flour, and vanilla. Beat until smooth. Add eggs and egg yolks, 1 at a time. Stir in whipping cream and lemon juice. Pour into crust.
4. Place springform pan on foil-lined baking sheet. Bake at 350° for 10 minutes. Reduce heat to 325° for 1 hour 20 minutes. Cool for 1 hour.
5. Stir together sour cream and ⅓ cup sugar; spread over cheesecake. Bake at 325° for 10 minutes. Cool. Cover and refrigerate 8 hours. Garnish with pralines.

FOOD FACTS

- Artichokes were first grown in Louisiana, brought there by settlers in the 1800s.
- Tabasco sauce was created on Avery Island, Louisiana, in 1868.
- Po'boys, sandwiches made with French bread and typically filled with fried oysters, shrimp, or crawfish, were created in New Orleans.

Maine

Lobster Casserole with Water Chestnuts and Bacon

1-2 cups cooked lobster meat
1/4 cup onion, finely chopped
1 green pepper, finely chopped
6-8 fresh mushrooms, sliced
1 can water chestnuts, sliced
1/2 cup chicken broth

1 egg yolk
1/2 cup all-purpose cream
1 tsp dry mustard
1 cup mayonnaise
1 cup cheddar cheese, grated
2 to 3 slices bacon, cooked and crumbled

1. Place lobster meat, onion, pepper, mushrooms, water chestnuts, and chicken broth in a frying pan. Bring to a boil and cook until vegetables are just tender. Spoon into 2-quart casserole dish.
2. Combine egg yolk and cream in a saucepan and cook slightly.
3. Add mustard and mayonnaise. Combine with casserole mixture. Top with grated cheese.
4. Bake at 350° for 15-20 minutes. Remove from oven and sprinkle with crumbled bacon.

Roasted Asparagus

1 lb fresh asparagus
2-3 T olive oil
1/4 tsp sugar

1/4 tsp salt
1/4 tsp pepper

1. Wash asparagus and break off tough ends.
2. Arrange in a single layer on a cookie sheet. Drizzle with olive oil.
3. Place oven rack on the closest rung to the broiler element. Broil asparagus 4-5 minutes.
4. Combine sugar, salt, and pepper in a small bowl. Sprinkle over asparagus.

Blueberry Pie

1 cup sugar
¼ cup all-purpose flour
¼ tsp nutmeg
⅛ tsp salt
4 cups fresh blueberries

1 T lemon juice
2 pie crusts
2 T butter
1 T sugar

1. Combine 1 cup sugar, flour, nutmeg, and salt in large bowl.
2. Add blueberries and lemon juice; toss.
3. Pour into bottom pie crust. Dot with butter.
4. Top with remaining pie crust. Fold and crimp edges. Cut slits in top crust. Sprinkle with sugar. Loosely tent edge with thin strips of foil to prevent overbrowning.
5. Bake at 425° for 10 minutes. Reduce heat to 375° for 30 minutes.

FOOD FACTS

- Early settlers in Maine actually got tired of eating lobster.
- Maine supplies 90% of the lobster consumed in the U.S.
- In 1848, chewing gum was invented in Bangor, Maine.
- Maine is the largest grower of wild blueberries in the world.

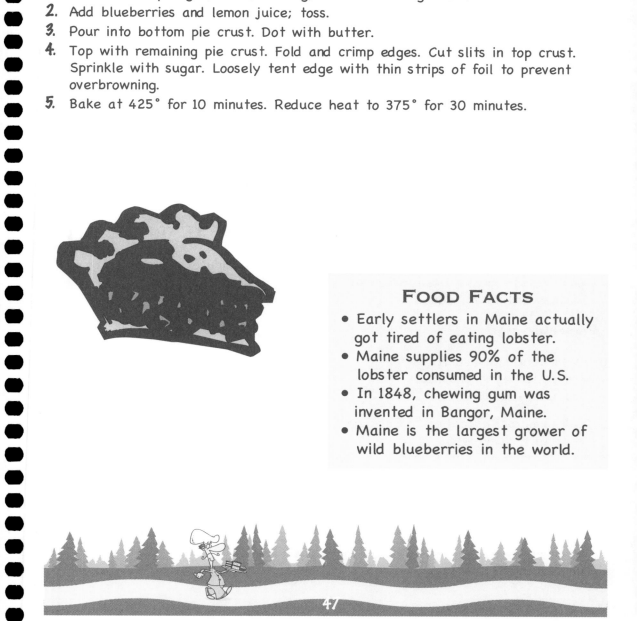

Maryland

These recipes come from my friend Heather, of Frederick, Maryland.

Crab Cakes

½ cup mayonnaise
1 egg, beaten
1 T Dijon mustard
1 T Worchestershire sauce

½ tsp hot sauce
1 lb fresh lump crabmeat
1 cup saltine cracker crumbs
oil

1. Drain crabmeat.
2. Mix together mayonnaise, egg, mustard, Worchestershire sauce, and hot sauce. Add in crab and crackers. Let stand 5 minutes.
3. Shape crab mixture into 8-10 cakes. Place on baking sheet or plate. Cover and chill at least 1 hour.
4. Heat oil over medium-high heat. Fry crab cakes 4 minutes on each side or until golden brown. Drain on paper towels. If desired, serve with lemon wedges and tartar sauce.

Macaroni Salad

16 oz large elbow macaroni
4 hard-boiled eggs, chopped
3-4 tomatoes, diced

2 cucumbers, diced
mayonnaise

1. Cook macaroni according to package directions, but omit salt; drain well.
2. In a large bowl, stir together macaroni, eggs, tomato, and cucumber.
3. Add mayonnaise to taste. You want the salad to be creamy.

*Do not add salt to salad as it breaks down the mayonnaise and makes it watery; salt and pepper individual servings to taste.

Pound Cake

1 cup milk
2 cups sugar
2 sticks butter, softened
3 cups flour

4 eggs
2 tsp vanilla
2 tsp baking powder
½ tsp salt

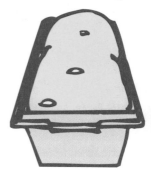

1. Cream sugar, eggs, butter, and vanilla.
2. Gradually add sifted flour and baking soda.
3. Add milk alternately.
4. Bake at 350° in a greased and floured loaf pan.

FOOD FACTS

- Over 50% of hard-shell crabs consumed in the U.S. come from the Chesapeake Bay.
- Maryland Blue Crab is the official state crustacean.
- Milk is the official state beverage.

Clam Chowder

5 cups bottled clam juice
1 stick margarine
1 cup finely diced celery
1 cup finely diced onion
½ cup cooked bacon, coarsely chopped
1 cup flour
3 6½-oz cans chopped clams

2 boiled potatoes
½ cup milk
½ cup light cream
1 tsp salt
black pepper, to taste
oyster crackers

1. In a large, thick-bottomed pan, heat the clam juice.
2. In a separate pan, melt margarine over medium-high heat. Add celery and onions and saute until they appear translucent (about 3 minutes).
3. Add bacon and flour and stir continuously for another 5 minutes. This mixture is your roux.
4. Increase heat on juice to medium-high, and with a wire whisk, add roux mixture to liquid. Stir constantly, and make sure to break up any lumps that may form.
5. Add clams (and the liquid that they are packed in) to chowder and stir.
6. Chop potatoes coarsely and add to chowder.
7. Add milk and light cream and stir. Add salt.
8. Decrease heat to medium-low. Simmer for about 20 minutes, stirring very frequently.
9. Serve piping hot with black pepper and oyster crackers.

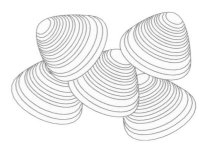

Boston Baked Beans

4 cup small white beans
2 onions
½ lb salt pork or fatty bacon
2 tsp dry mustard

1 cup molasses
½ tsp pepper
2 tsp salt
2-4 cups hot water

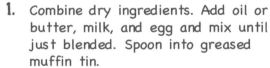

1. Soak the beans in cold water for 12-24 hours.
2. Cut the onions in quarters and throw them into the bottom of the bean pot. Add the drained beans. Stir in the salt pork.
3. Mix all of the other ingredients with 2-4 cups of hot water; stir into the beans.
4. Add enough water to cover the beans, and put the pot in 250° oven.
   Cook 6-8 hours, adding water as necessary and occasionally stirring the beans. For the last hour or so you can leave the pot uncovered to get rid of some excess water.

Corn Muffins

1 cup cornmeal
1 cup flour
2-4 T sugar
4 tsp baking powder

½ tsp salt
¼ cup oil or butter, melted
1 cup milk
1 egg, beaten

1. Combine dry ingredients. Add oil or butter, milk, and egg and mix until just blended. Spoon into greased muffin tin.
2. Bake at 400° for 18-20 minutes or until golden brown.

Massachusetts

Boston Cream Pie

1¾ cups flour (if using all-purpose flour, decrease the amount by 2 T)

½ tsp salt	½ tsp vanilla
2 tsp baking powder	2 eggs
⅓ cup butter	½ cup milk

1. Preheat the oven to 375°. Sift together flour, salt, and baking powder in a bowl.
2. Cream the butter. Add vanilla and gradually beat in sugar. Beat until fluffy. Beat in 2 eggs and stir in ½ cup flour mixture.
3. Stir in ¼ cup milk and then add ½ cup flour mixture and another ¼ cup milk. Mix. Add the rest of the flour mixture and beat just enough to blend well.
4. Spoon the batter into 2 greased and floured 7- or 8-inch round cake pans.
5. Bake the layers 20-30 minutes at 375°. Cool 10 minutes; remove from pans. Cool completely.

Cream Filling:

½ cup sugar	1 cup milk
3 T flour or 1 T cornstarch	1 egg or 2 egg yolks (slightly beaten)
few grains salt	½ tsp vanilla

1. Put the sugar, flour, and salt in a small heavy saucepan. Stir in milk. Cook over low heat, stirring constantly, until the mixture thickens (about 5 minutes).
2. Add the 1 egg or 2 egg yolks and mix. Cook and stir for 3 more minutes. Stir in vanilla. Chill.

Chocolate Frosting:

2 ounces unsweetened chocolate	2 cups confectioners sugar
1 T butter	½ tsp vanilla
½ cup milk	

1. Place chocolate, butter, and milk in the top of a double boiler. Cook on medium low until the chocolate melts. Stir well.
2. Take off the heat and let stand until lukewarm. Stir in sugar and vanilla. Beat until thick enough to spread.

Put together the cream pie:

Put the layers together with cream filling. Spread with chocolate frosting.

FOOD FACTS

- When the French arrived in New England, they brought with them their traditional thick soup of seafood and vegetables called chowder.
- Parker House rolls were accidentally created by the baker at Boston's Parker House Hotel.
- At the Toll House Inn in Whitman, Massachusetts, the innkeeper's wife added chocolate pieces to her cookies and called them Toll House cookies. The chocolate chip cookie is the official state cookie.
- Boston Cream Pie is the official state dessert.
- The corn muffin is the official state muffin.
- The cranberry was made the official state berry of Massachusetts in 1994.
- Cranberry juice is the official state beverage of Massachusetts.
- In 1993, the navy bean was made the official vegetable.
- Quincy is home to the first Dunkin Donuts.
- The first recorded planting of apple seeds was in 1629 by the Massachusetts Bay Colony.
- Established in 1847, the New England Confectionery Company (NECCO) is the oldest candy company in the United States. In 1866, Daniel Chase invented the Lozenge Printing Machine, creating "conversation candies," which had instant and widespread popularity. NECCO is the #1 maker of the famous Valentine conversation hearts with romantic words and messages stamped on them.
- In 1891, Fig Newtons were created at the Kennedy Biscuit Works in Cambridgeport, Massachusetts.

Michigan

My chiropractor, a native Michigander, told me this would be a typical Michigan home-style meal.

Meat Loaf

1½ pounds ground beef
2 eggs
¾ cup milk
½ cup dry breadcrumbs
⅛ tsp pepper
2 tsp onion powder

2 tsp parsley
1 tsp salt
½ tsp sage
¼ cup ketchup
2 T brown sugar
1 tsp dry mustard

1. Mix first 9 ingredients together and form into a loaf.
2. Place in loaf pan and bake 1 hour 15 minutes at 350°.
3. Combine ketchup, brown sugar, and mustard.
4. Spread over meat loaf and return to oven for 10 minutes.

Crock-Pot Macaroni and Cheese

8 oz macaroni
1 large can evaporated milk
½ cup milk
1 tsp salt

¼ cup melted butter
1 egg, beaten
12 oz shredded cheddar cheese
paprika

1. Cook macaroni 6-7 minutes; drain.
2. Reserve ½ cup cheese.
3. Combine all ingredients in a buttered Crock-Pot.
4. Top with reserved cheese. Sprinkle with paprika.
5. Cook 3¼ hours on low.

Cherry Cobbler

6 cups pitted fresh cherries
1½ cups sugar
3 T cornstarch
½ cup water
3 T butter, softened
1 T lemon juice
¼ tsp almond extract

1 cup all-purpose flour
1 tsp baking powder
½ tsp salt
½ cup milk
¼ cup butter
1 tsp vanilla
1 egg

1. Boil cherries, ¾ cup sugar, cornstarch, and water for 1 minute, stirring constantly. Remove from heat.
2. Stir in 3 T butter, lemon juice, and almond extract.
3. Pour into 11x7-inch baking dish, lightly coated with cooking spray.
4. Combine remaining ¾ cup sugar, flour, baking powder, and salt in mixing bowl.
5. Add milk, ¼ cup butter, and vanilla; beat for 2 minutes on medium.
6. Add egg and beat additional 2 minutes.
7. Spoon over cherry mixture.
8. Bake at 350° for 40 minutes or until golden brown.

FOOD FACTS

- Michigan is the country's leading grower of cherries.
- Battle Creek, Michigan, is home to Kellogg's, Post, and Ralston Purina cereal companies.
- The first soda pop made in the U.S. was Vernor's Ginger Ale, created in Detroit, Michigan, in 1866.
- Michigan's key agrigultural products are dairy products, apples, blueberries, cattle, vegetables, hogs, corn, nursery stock, soybeans.

Minnesota

Minnesota has two casserole recipes because I couldn't decide between the two since they both bring back special memories of our year there.

Tater Tot Casserole

$1/2$–1 lb ground beef
1 can cream of mushroom soup
milk (use 1 soup can to measure)

2 cans French-cut green beans, drained
1 can cream of chicken soup
frozen tater tots

1. Brown ground beef; drain.
2. In 9x13-inch pan, combine all ingredients except tater tots. Add salt and pepper to taste. Cover with a single layer of tater tots.
3. Bake uncovered at 350° for 45 minutes or until bubbly and tater tots are browned.

Chicken and Wild Rice Casserole

1 6-oz box wild rice
2 cups chicken, cooked and chopped
1 can cream of mushroom soup
3-oz can mushrooms, drained

1 cup grated cheddar cheese
1 T lemon juice
salt and pepper to taste

1. Cook rice according to package directions.
2. Combine rice, chicken, and $1/2$ cup grated cheese. Stir in lemon juice and salt and pepper.
3. Spoon into casserole dish.
4. Top with soup, mushrooms, then remaining cheese.
5. Bake at 325° for 30 minutes.

Star of the North Bars

1 stick butter, melted
3/4-1 cup graham cracker crumbs
1 T sugar
1 cup light corn syrup
2/3 cup butter
1 cup peanut butter

2 cups oatmeal
1 cup packed brown sugar
1/2 cup plain flour
6 oz semisweet chocolate chips
shredded coconut

1. Combine melted butter, graham cracker crumbs, and 1 T sugar. Press into bottom of 9x13-inch pan.
2. Bring corn syrup to a boil. Add 2/3 cup butter and peanut butter, stirring constantly until blended. Stir in oatmeal, brown sugar, and flour. Spread on crust.
4. Sprinkle with chocolate chips. Put in 325° oven until chocolate is melted. Remove from oven and spread chocolate with knife. Sprinkle with coconut to taste.
6. Return to oven until coconut is toasted golden brown.

FOOD FACTS

- Minnesota is the country's leading producer of wild rice, which is the state's official grain.
- General Mills, which owns Pillsbury, Betty Crocker, and Green Giant, is headquartered in Minneapolis. Pillsbury and Green Giant were both started in Minnesota.
- Austin, Minnesota, is home to the Hormel Company's plant that produces Spam.
- Patrick Towle, a St. Paul grocer, invented Log Cabin syrup.
- Wheaties cereal, Bisquick, and the bundt pan were all invented in Minnesota.
- Alexander Anderson of Red Wing, Minnesota, developed the processes to create puffed wheat and puffed rice.
- Frank C. Mars of Minnesota created the Milky Way candy bar in 1923. The Snickers candy bar, introduced in 1930, was named after a horse owned by the Mars family.

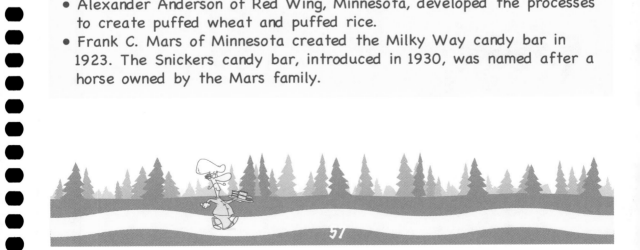

Mississippi

Chicken and Dumplings

This is my specialty. My husband calls this "the stuff legends are made of."

2-4 split chicken breasts   ¼ cup chicken bouillon
½-1 tsp pepper

1. Boil chicken in approximately 8 cups water for 1 hour.
2. Remove chicken from pot to cool; add bouillon and pepper to broth.
3. Remove chicken from bone and shred. Return to pot.
4. Bring broth to a boil.
5. Drop dough rectangles, 1 at a time, into boiling broth. Gently stir occasionally.
6. Reduce heat to simmer for 20 minutes. Stir often.
7. If necessary, add a little flour to thicken broth.

Dumplings:

2 cups all-purpose flour   1 T baking powder
½ tsp salt   ¼ cup shortening
⅔-¾ cup milk

1. Combine dry ingredients.
2. Cut in shortening until crumbly.
3. Add milk and blend.
4. Turn dough onto lightly floured surface; knead 3 or 4 times.
5. Roll out dough and sprinkle with flour. (The key to good dumplings is rolling the dough very thin.)
6. Cut into 1x½-inch rectangles.

Fried Green Tomatoes

3 slices of bacon
4 medium green tomatoes
1 cup fine ground cornmeal

salt and pepper to taste
$\frac{1}{2}$ cup milk

1. Fry bacon in heavy skillet. Mix together cornmeal, salt, and pepper.
2. Dip $\frac{1}{2}$-inch tomato slices in milk; dredge with cornmeal mixture.
3. Fry tomatoes in the bacon fat over medium heat until the cornmeal browns, about $1\frac{1}{2}$ minutes on each side.

Mississippi Mud

This is another of my Nanny's recipes and my all-time favorite childhood dessert. To this day, no one makes it like Nanny did.

2 sticks butter, melted
$\frac{1}{2}$ cup cocoa
4 eggs, beaten
1 tsp vanilla

2 cups sugar
$1\frac{1}{2}$ cups flour
1 tsp salt
$1\frac{1}{2}$ cups pecans

1. Preheat oven to 350°.
2. Blend butter and cocoa. Add eggs, vanilla, and sugar.
4. Mix in flour and salt. Stir in pecans.
6. Bake for 35 minutes in a greased 9x13-inch pan.
7. Remove from oven. Add single layer of miniature marshmallows. Return to oven for a few minutes to melt marshmallows.
8. Cool.

Frosting:

1 lb powdered sugar
$\frac{1}{2}$ cup milk
$\frac{1}{2}$ cup cocoa
1 stick butter, melted

Blend ingredients and frost cake.

FOOD FACTS

- Borden's Condensed Milk was first canned in Liberty, Mississippi.
- The first football player on a Wheaties cereal box was Walter Payton of Columbia, Mississippi.
- Mississippi's key agricultural products are cotton, poultry, cattle, catfish, soybeans, dairy products, and rice.

Chili Mac

12 oz elbow macaroni
2 T oil
2 T flour
2 cups milk
1 T onion powder

1 tsp salt
$\frac{1}{8}$ tsp cayenne pepper
1 cup shredded cheddar cheese
4 cups chili

1. Cook and drain macaroni.
2. Heat oil in saucepan; stir in flour. Whisk in milk. Cook and stir until thickened.
3. Stir in onion powder, salt, cayenne pepper, and $\frac{1}{2}$ cup cheese. Remove from heat.
4. Stir in macaroni.
5. Spoon into 9x13-inch pan.
6. Top with chili. Sprinkle with $\frac{1}{2}$ cup cheese.
7. Bake, covered, at 375° until hot and bubbly.

Creamed Corn

An old family recipe that I had to make in order to get the measurements right.

12 ears of corn
$\frac{1}{2}$ cup evaporated milk

3 T butter
salt

1. Cut off tips of corn kernels into large bowl with a sharp knife; scrape each cob twice with a table knife. Pour into baking dish.
2. Add remaining ingredients.
3. Bake at 350° for 30 minutes, stirring every 10 minutes.

Gooey Butter Cake

1 yellow cake mix   1 egg
1 stick butter, melted   ⅓ cup sugar

Mix all ingredients together and press into a 9x13-inchpan.

Icing

1 lb powdered sugar   1 egg
8 oz cream cheese

1. Set aside ½ cup powdered sugar.
2. Mix remaining sugar with cream cheese and egg. Spread on cake layer.
3. Sprinkle with reserved powdered sugar.
4. Bake at 350° for 25 minutes.

FOOD FACTS

- Missouri is the country's leading grower of black walnuts.
- The official state nut is the walnut.
- Soybeans are Missouri's largest cash crop.
- Ice cream cones were invented when an ice cream vendor at the 1904 St. Louis World's Fair ran out of clean dishes. Near his booth was a vendor selling wafer-thin Persian waffles. Waffles were rolled into cones and filled with ice cream.
- The Campbell's Soup kids were first introduced at the St. Louis World's Fair.
- Aunt Jemima pancake flour was the first ready-mix food to be sold commercially. It was invented in St. Joseph, Missouri.
- One of Mark Twain's favorite meals was pan-fried porterhouse steak with mushrooms and peas.

Montana

Montana Special

3 pound venison or beef roast
salt and pepper
garlic salt
flour
oil or shortening

1 can tomatoes
1 can tomato hot sauce
1 large onion
1 cup water

1. Trim the roast of fat and slice as thin as possible. Sprinkle salt, pepper, and garlic on both sides of each piece of the roast. Dredge in flour.
2. Heat enough oil or shortening to cover the bottom of frying pan.
3. Brown on both sides. Put the pieces in a roaster or covered pan.
4. Put remaining ingredients over the top the roast and bake in the oven at 300° for about 3 hours or until done.

Zucchini Casserole

4 cups water
6 cups sliced zucchini
1 cup shredded carrots
1/4 cup chopped onion
1 tsp salt
1 can cream of mushroom soup

1 cup sour cream
1/2 tsp garlic powder
1/2 tsp pepper
4 cups seasoned stuffing croutons
1/2 cup butter, melted

1. Bring water to boil; add zucchini, carrots, onion, and salt. Cook until vegetables are tender; drain.
2. In a large bowl, combine soup, sour cream, garlic powder, and pepper. Fold in vegetable mixture.
3. Combine croutons and butter; place half in greased 9x13-inch baking dish. Top with vegetable mixture and remaining croutons.
4. Cover and bake at 350° for 30 minutes. Uncover; bake 10 minutes longer.

Huckleberry Cake

1½ cups sifted flour
1 tsp baking powder
¼ tsp salt
½ cup butter
1 cup sugar

2 eggs, separated
1 tsp vanilla
⅓ cup milk
1½ cups huckleberries

1. Sift together dry ingredients, except sugar.
2. Beat ½ cup butter until creamy; add 1 cup sugar and beat until fluffy.
3. Beat in egg yolks and vanilla until light and creamy.
4. Add sifted dry ingredients alternately with the milk.
5. Fold in beaten egg whites.
6. Fold in berries.
7. Turn into a greased 8x8-inch pan. Sprinkle top of the batter lightly with granulated sugar.
8. Bake at 350° for 50-60 minutes.

FOOD FACTS

- In Montana, there are four times as many cattle as there are people.
- During the summer and fall, wild huckleberries grow abundantly in Montana. No one has yet succeeded in growing huckleberries commercially. Because of this, huckleberries are a true "natural food" with no fertilizers or pesticides.
- Many people use the name "huckleberry" to identify wild blueberries. Huckleberries are related to blueberries, but are quite different. Blueberries are blue to dark blue and have many small, soft, barely-noticeable seeds; huckleberries are blackish blue or red-black (a kind of a purple color) and have large seeds that are much tougher.
- Montana's main crop is wheat; nationwide, the state ranks fifth in wheat production.

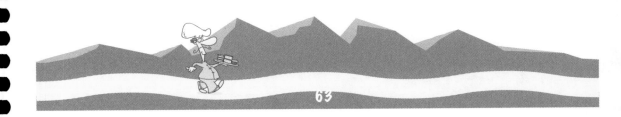

Nebraska

This is typical tailgate fare at a Cornhusker football game.

Runza

2 loaves frozen bread dough
1 lb ground beef
½ head cabbage, chopped

½ medium onion, chopped
salt and pepper to taste

1. Thaw frozen bread dough or make the equivalent amount using your favorite bread recipe. While dough thaws, make the filling.
2. Brown ground beef and drain, then return to pan.
3. Add cabbage and onion and cook down. Salt and pepper to taste.
4. Let dough rise, then punch down and roll a portion to ¼-inch thickness. Cut into 4x8-inch pieces and add about ½ cup meat mixture to each.
5. Fold dough pieces over and seal the edges, then place seam-side down on a greased cookie sheet.
6. Let rise 20-30 minutes; then bake in a 375° oven for 20 minutes or until brown.

Zesty Pasta Salad

12 oz tricolor twist pasta
1 roasted red pepper, chopped
1 can sliced black olives, drained

1 can diced tomatoes, drained
1 12-oz bottle house Italian dressing
shredded mozzarella cheese

1. Cook, rinse, and drain pasta.
2. Combine all ingredients except cheese.
3. Cover and chill.
4. Serve with cheese to taste.

To roast pepper:
1. Wash, seed, and cut pepper in half.
2. Place on foil-lined baking pan and flatten halves with palm.
3. Place on oven rack closest to broiler element. Broil until blistered.
4. Seal peppers immediately in Ziploc bag. Allow to set for 10-15 minutes to loosen skin. Remove skin.

Nebraska Raisin Bars

1¾ cups all-purpose flour
¼ tsp salt
1 tsp baking soda
1 tsp ground cinnamon
½ tsp ground nutmeg
½ tsp ground allspice
½ tsp ground cloves
1 cup raisins

1 cup apple juice
½ cup butter
1 egg, beaten
1 tsp vanilla
1 cup sugar
½ cup chopped walnuts
¼ cup powdered sugar

1. Preheat oven to 375°.
2. Grease and flour a 10x15-inch baking pan.
3. Sift together flour, salt, baking soda, cinnamon, nutmeg, allspice, and cloves.
4. Combine raisins and juice in saucepan and bring to a boil. Remove from heat and stir in butter. Cool.
5. When the mixture has cooled to lukewarm, beat in egg and vanilla.
6. Mix in sugar; stir to blend. Beat in flour mixture. Stir in walnuts.
7. Pour into prepared baking pan.
8. Bake for 12 minutes. When cool, sprinkle lightly with powdered sugar.

FOOD FACTS

- Kool-Aid was invented in Nebraska by Edwin Perkins and is the official state soft drink.
- Milk is the official state beverage.
- The Reuben sandwich was invented in Omaha.
- ConAgra Foods, one of the largest food companies in the world, is headquartered in Grand Island, Nebraska.
- In Blue Hill, Nebraska, no female wearing a "hat that would scare a timid person" can be seen eating onions in public.
- Runza sandwiches are popular in Nebraska. The first Runza Drive-In opened in Lincoln in 1949.

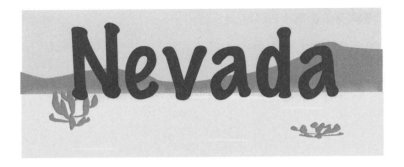

Baked Chicken with Noodles

4½-lb chicken
1 package chicken Bag-n-Season
1 cup water
10 oz egg noodles
6 T butter

3 cloves garlic, minced
1 tsp salt
2 T parsley
2 T grated Parmesan cheese

1. Preheat oven 325°. Cut chicken in half. Place the halves skin side up in the plastic baking bag included in the Bag-n-Season package and sprinkle the seasoning mix over both halves.
2. Pour water gently into the bag. Tie off end of bag and poke 1 or 2 small holes in the center of the top. Bake for 1 hour.
3. After about 45 minutes, start boiling noodles so that they will be cooked and draining as the chicken is finished baking. Do not rinse.
4. Remove chicken from bag.
5. Pour at least 1 cup of drippings into saucepan along with butter, garlic, salt, and parsley.
6. Gently fold in noodles, then sprinkle on Parmesan cheese and cook over medium heat, stirring gently until the sauce begins to thicken.
7. Arrange noodles on platter around chicken.

Stuffed Mushrooms

2 packages frozen spinach, thawed
²/₃ cup sour cream
½ cup cheddar cheese
½ cup Monterey Jack cheese
¼ cup Parmesan cheese

¼ cup green onion tops, chopped
1 tsp salt
1 tsp Italian seasoning
12 giant mushrooms

1. Squeeze excess water from spinach.
2. Mix with remaining ingredients, except mushrooms.
3. Remove stems from mushrooms.
4. Place cup side up, in center of large baking dish. Fill with spinach mixture.
5. Bake, uncovered, at 350° for 25 minutes.

Toffee Cake

1 German chocolate cake mix
1 can sweetened condensed milk
6 Heath candy bars, crushed

1 jar caramel sauce
8 oz non-dairy whipped topping

1. Bake cake according to directions in a 9x13-inch pan.
2. Immediately after removing cake from oven, punch holes in cake with a straw or handle of a wooden spoon; pour sweetened condensed milk then caramel sauce over cake.
3. Cool completely and top with whipped topping. Sprinkle crushed Heath bars over top.

FOOD FACTS

- The state grass is Indian rice-grass. It was eaten by Native Americans and early pioneers.
- Nevada's main crops are alfalfa, onion, garlic, grains, and potatoes.
- Nevada's key agricultural products are cattle, hay, dairy products, and potatoes.

New Hampshire

Roasted Corn Chowder

8 ears of corn
2 large potatoes
8 cups vegetable stock
salt and pepper

onion powder
celery salt
1 cup milk
2 roasted orange peppers

1. Pull husks back from corn, remove silks, and pull husks back up to cover. Place on a baking sheet and roast in 450° oven for 30 minutes. Cool. Remove husks. Cut kernels from cobs. Set aside.
2. Peel and dice potatoes. Place in large stockpot with vegetable stock, and spices (to taste). Bring to a boil. Reduce heat and simmer 30 minutes. Add corn. Simmer for additional 15 minutes.
3. Ladle 4 cups of soup into blender or food processor. Allow to cool slightly.
4. While this is cooling, roast peppers. Remove tops of peppers, seed, wash, and cut in half. Place on cookie sheet and flatten with palm. Place under broiler (oven rack should be as close to broiler element as possible) until skins are well blistered. Put in a Ziploc bag and seal. Set aside for 15 minutes to loosen skins. Remove skins.
5. Place roasted peppers in blender or food processor with the 4 cups of soup. Blend. Pour back into stockpot. Add milk.

Whole Wheat Bread

2 packets dried yeast
3 cups warm water
2 T honey
1 cup white flour

6-7 cups whole wheat flour
3 T oil
1 T salt
1 egg and 1 T milk, beaten

1. Dissolve yeast in water in a large bowl. Add honey, white flour, and 2 cups of whole wheat flour. Beat vigorously with a spoon to form a smooth batter. Cover and set aside to rise in a warm place for 40 minutes.
2. Stir in oil and salt, then fold in about 3½ cups whole wheat flour, ½ cup at a time, rotating the bowl a quarter of a turn between folds. When the dough is too thick to add any more flour, turn onto a floured work surface and knead 5-8 minutes, adding only enough flour to make smooth elastic dough.

3. Place dough in an oiled bowl and turn it over so that the top is coated with oil. Cover and let rise in a warm place for about 45 minutes until doubled in size.
4. Punch the dough down and leave for a further 35 minutes or so to rise again.
5. Shape the dough into 2 loaves and let them rise in the oiled pans for a further 30 minutes until doubled in size.
6. Preheat oven to 350°. Brush the tops of the loaves with the egg wash. Bake for about 1 hour or until browned. Remove from oven and turn onto rack to cool.

Orange Cake

1 package yellow cake mix
1/2 cup vegetable oil
1 tsp vanilla

1 cup fresh orange juice
1/4 cup sugar
4 large eggs

1. Preheat oven to 350°. Lightly spray a 12-cup Bundt pan with cooking spray, then dust with flour, shaking out excess. Set aside.
2. Place the cake mix, orange juice, oil, sugar, vanilla, and eggs in a large mixing bowl. Blend on low speed for 1 minute. Increase speed to medium and beat 2 more minutes, occasionally scraping down the sides of the bowl. The batter should look thick and well blended.
3. Pour batter into prepared pan and place on middle rack of oven. Bake until cake is golden brown and starts to pull away from the sides of the pan, 45 to 50 minutes.
4. Remove from oven and cool for 20 minutes. Remove from pan and cool completely.

Glaze

1 cup powdered sugar, sifted
3 T fresh orange juice
1 tsp fresh grated orange zest

1. Combine the sugar, juice, and zest in a small bowl and stir until smooth.
2. Place the cake on a serving platter and pour the glaze over the top, letting it drizzle down the sides.
3. Let the glaze set a few minutes before slicing.

FOOD FACTS

- Potatoes were first introduced to the New World in 1719 through colonists arriving in New Hampshire.
- Earl Tupper of Berlin, New Hampshire, invented Tupperware® and founded Tupper Plastics Company in 1938.
- New Hampshire grows a variety of berries, apples, and pumpkins.
- You may not tap your feet, nod your head, or in any way keep time to the music in a restaurant or cafe in New Hampshire.

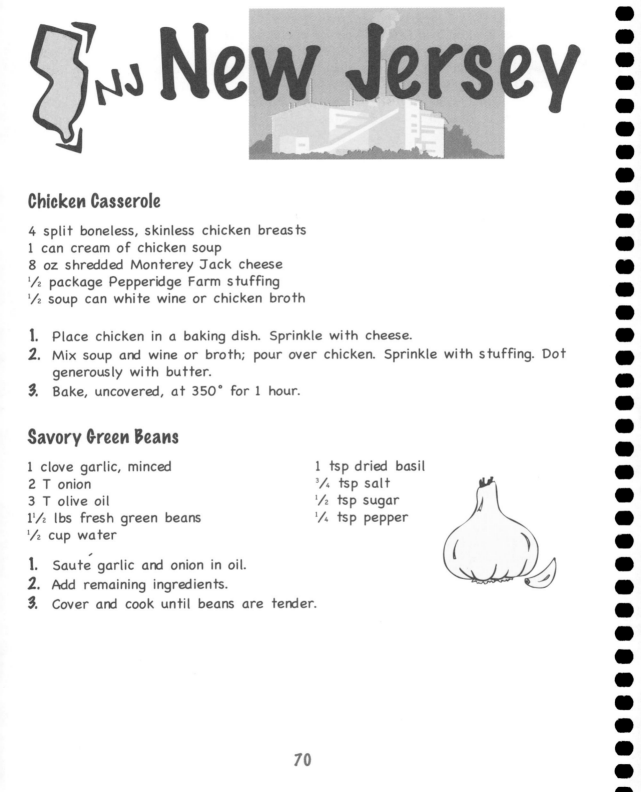

New Jersey

Chicken Casserole

4 split boneless, skinless chicken breasts
1 can cream of chicken soup
8 oz shredded Monterey Jack cheese
½ package Pepperidge Farm stuffing
½ soup can white wine or chicken broth

1. Place chicken in a baking dish. Sprinkle with cheese.
2. Mix soup and wine or broth; pour over chicken. Sprinkle with stuffing. Dot generously with butter.
3. Bake, uncovered, at 350° for 1 hour.

Savory Green Beans

1 clove garlic, minced
2 T onion
3 T olive oil
1½ lbs fresh green beans
½ cup water

1 tsp dried basil
¾ tsp salt
½ tsp sugar
¼ tsp pepper

1. Sauté garlic and onion in oil.
2. Add remaining ingredients.
3. Cover and cook until beans are tender.

Blueberry Cobbler

1½ cups flour	2¼ tsp baking soda
¼ tsp salt	6 T butter
1½ T sugar	¾ cup heavy cream

1. Sift the dry ingredients together, then cut the butter into the mixture.
2. Add the heavy cream, but do not overmix.

4½ cups blueberries	1 T flour
⅓ cup sugar	

1. Toss all the filling ingredients together so they are well mixed.
2. Place the berry mixture in a buttered and sugared baking dish.
3. Roll the dough out to cover the dish and place over the fruit.
4. Bake at 375° for 35-40 minutes.

FOOD FACTS

- Campbell's Soup Company was founded in New Jersey in 1869. In 1897, John Dorrance performed an experiment that resulted in condensed soup. Because it lowered shipping costs, this new technology gave the company a distinct advantage over its competitors.
- Milk was first pasteurized in Princeton, New Jersey, in 1904.
- New Jersey has more diners than any other state and is sometimes called the "diner capital of the world."
- New Jersey is the country's leading grower of green beans.

New Mexico

Chicken in the Chips

2½ cups cooked chicken, diced
1 can cream of chicken soup
½ cup sour cream

½ cup salsa
2 cups Monterey Jack cheese
2 cups corn chips

1. Combine chicken, soup, sour cream, and salsa; mix well.
2. Spoon half the mixture into a 1½-quart baking dish. Top with 1 cup cheese and 1 cup chips. Repeat layers.
3. Bake uncovered at 350° for 25 minutes.

Southwest Beans

1 lb dried pinto beans
8 cups water
1 onion, chopped
1 red or green bell pepper, chopped
1-2 cloves garlic, minced
2 T Worchestershire sauce

1 T chili powder
¾ tsp salt
½ tsp dry mustard
¼ tsp pepper
10-oz can tomatoes and green chiles

1. Soak beans at least 6 hours. Drain.
2. Bring beans and water to a boil. Cover, reduce heat, and simmer for 1 hour or until tender.
3. Add all remaining ingredients except tomatoes and simmer ½-1 hour.
4. Add tomatoes and simmer ½ hour.

Milky Way Cake

8 1⅞-oz Milky Way candy bars
½ cup butter, melted
2 cups sugar
½ cup butter, softened
4 eggs

1 tsp vanilla
1¼ cups buttermilk
½ tsp baking soda
3 cups all-purpose flour
1 cup chopped pecans
chocolate frosting

1. Combine candy bars and melted butter in saucepan. Cook over low heat until candy bars are melted, stirring constantly; cool.
2. Cream sugar and softened butter until light and fluffy.
3. Add eggs, 1 at a time, beating after each addition. Stir in vanilla.
4. Combine buttermilk and baking soda; add to creamed mixture alternately with flour, beating after each addition.
5. Stir in melted candy bars and pecans.
6. Pour into a greased and floured tube pan.
7. Bake at 325° for 1 hour 20 minutes or until toothpick comes out clean.
8. Cool 1 hour. Remove from pan and cool completely.
9. Frost with your favorite chocolate frosting recipe.

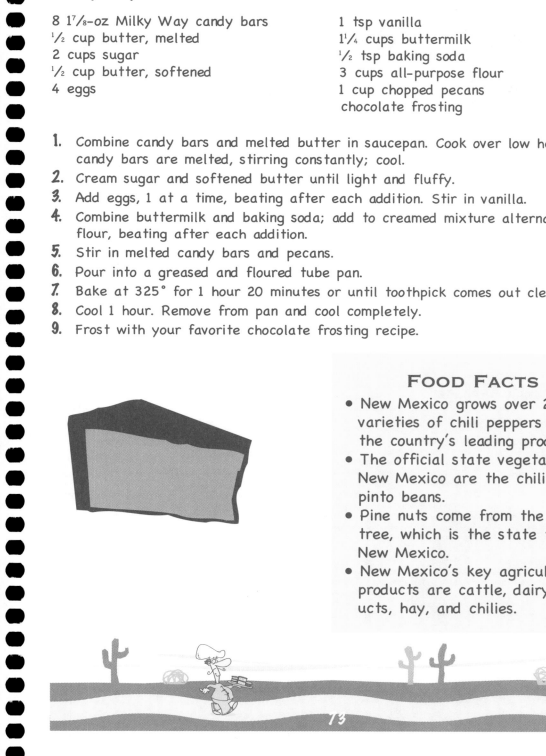

FOOD FACTS

- New Mexico grows over 200 varieties of chili peppers and is the country's leading producer.
- The official state vegetables of New Mexico are the chili and pinto beans.
- Pine nuts come from the piñon tree, which is the state tree of New Mexico.
- New Mexico's key agricultural products are cattle, dairy products, hay, and chilies.

New York

Chicken and Noodles

8–10 cups chicken broth
1 lb egg noodles
1 lb chicken, cooked and shredded

1. Bring broth to a boil. Add noodles and chicken; simmer 10 minutes.
2. Cover and let stand for 20 minutes. Salt and pepper to taste.

Baked Creamed Cabbage

1 medium head cabbage
$\frac{1}{2}$ cup boiling salted water
3 T butter
3 T flour

$\frac{1}{2}$ tsp salt
$1\frac{1}{2}$ cups milk
$\frac{1}{4}$ cup breadcrumbs

1. Shred cabbage and cook 9 minutes in boiling, salted water. Remove cabbage, drain well, and place in buttered $1\frac{1}{2}$-quart casserole dish.
2. Melt butter in pan; stir in flour and salt; cook until smooth. Add milk gradually. Continue stirring until thick.
3. Pour sauce over cabbage and sprinkle breadcrumbs over top.
4. Bake at 325° for 15 minutes or until crumbs are browned.

Red Velvet Cake

½ cup butter
1½ cups sugar
2 eggs
2 T cocoa
2 oz red food coloring
2½ cups cake flour
1 tsp salt

4 tsp baking powder
1 cup buttermilk
3 tsp vanilla
¼ cup water
1 tsp baking soda
1 tsp vinegar

1. Cream butter and sugar until fluffy. Add eggs and beat well. Add cocoa and food coloring.
2. Sift flour, salt, and baking powder; add to batter alternately with buttermilk, vanilla, and water. Add baking soda and blend well. Gently stir in vinegar.
3. Pour into 2 greased and floured round cake pans. Bake at 350° for 30 minutes. Cool for 10 minutes; remove from pans. Cool completely. Frost.

Frosting:
5 T flour
1 cup milk
1 cup butter, softened
1 cup sugar
1 tsp vanilla

1. Cook flour and milk to a thick paste. Cool, then chill in refrigerator.
2. Cream together butter, sugar, and vanilla.
3. Add chilled paste.

FOOD FACTS
- In 1853, Chef George Crum invented potato chips at Moon's Lake House in Saratoga Springs, New York. They were originally called Saratoga Chips.
- Henry Perky invented shredded wheat cereal in Watertown, New York, in 1892.
- Red Velvet Cake was created at the Waldorf-Astoria Hotel in New York City around 1900.
- Gennaro Lombardi's, an Italian restaurant in New York City, served America's first pizza in 1905.
- New York is the leading grower of cabbage.

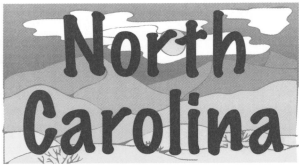

North Carolina

Country Style Steak

My boys love this recipe!

4-6 cube steaks
flour
salt and pepper
oil

2 dry beefy mushroom soup pouches
2 cans condensed beefy mushroom soup
2 soup cans measure of milk

1. Dredge cube steaks in flour seasoned with salt and pepper.
2. Brown in hot oil for 2-3 minutes per side. Place in baking dish.
3. Mix mushroom soup pouches, beefy mushroom soup, and milk. Pour over steaks.
4. Bake, covered, at 350° until bubbly. Reduce heat to 250° and bake for 2 hours.

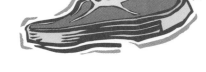

Serve with mashed potatoes.

Squash Casserole

2 lbs sliced yellow squash
2 tsp onion powder
2 T butter, melted
1 1/2 cups cheddar cheese
1/4 tsp salt

2 eggs, beaten
4 slices cooked bacon, crumbled
1 1/4 cups Ritz cracker crumbs
1/4 tsp pepper

1. Reserve 1/2 cup cracker crumbs.
2. Boil squash for 10 minutes. Drain well and mash.
3. Combine with all ingredients except 1/2 cup cracker crumbs.
4. Spoon into baking dish. Sprinkle with reserved cracker crumbs.
5. Bake, uncovered, at 350° for 45 minutes.

Four-Layer Delight

It is rare to attend a covered dish dinner in our part of North Carolina where some variation of this dessert is not present. Coconut, vanilla, chocolate, or butterscotch pudding can be substituted for the lemon pudding.

Layer 1: Mix together 1 cup butter, 1 cup chopped pecans, and 2 cups all-purpose flour. Spread in the bottom of 9x13-inch pan. Bake at 350° for 25 minutes. Cool completely.

Layer 2: Mix together 8 oz cream cheese and 1 cup powdered sugar. Fold in 1 cup non-dairy whipped topping. Spread on cooled crust.

Layer 3: Beat 2 small packages lemon pudding mix with 3 cups cold milk. Spread on top of cream cheese layer.

Layer 4: Top with remainder of 16 oz tub of non-dairy whipped topping. Refrigerate.

Zucchini Bread

2 cups shredded raw zucchini
3 eggs
1¾ cups sugar
1 cup oil
2 cups flour
¼ tsp baking powder

2 tsp baking soda
2 tsp cinnamon
1 tsp salt
2 tsp vanilla
1 cup chopped nuts

1. Put zucchini in strainer and press or squeeze to get excess liquid out.
2. Beat eggs, sugar, and oil together. Add flour, baking powder, soda, cinnamon, salt, vanilla, and nuts. Stir by hand.
3. Add zucchini (minus liquid). Mix well.
4. Pour into 2 greased, floured, loaf pans. Bake 1 hour at 350°.

FOOD FACTS

- In 1895, Pepsi was invented in New Bern, North Carolina.
- North Carolina is the country's leading producer of turkeys and sweet potatoes.
- Rose Hill, North Carolina, is home to the world's largest frying pan. The 15-foot-wide pan can hold up to 200 gallons of oil and fry 365 chickens at one time.
- The sweet potato is the official state vegetable.

Dakota Bread

1 package active dry yeast
$\frac{1}{2}$ cup warm water (105-110°)
2 T sunflower oil
1 egg
$\frac{1}{2}$ cup cottage cheese
$\frac{1}{4}$ cup honey
1 tsp salt
2-$2\frac{1}{2}$ cups bread flour
$\frac{1}{2}$ cup whole wheat flour
$\frac{1}{4}$ cup wheat germ
$\frac{1}{4}$ cup rye flour
$\frac{1}{4}$ cup rolled oats
cornmeal

1. Sprinkle yeast in warm water; stir to dissolve.
2. In a large bowl, mix sunflower oil, egg, cottage cheese, honey, and salt. Add dissolved yeast and 2 cups bread flour, beating until flour is moistened. Gradually stir in whole wheat flour, wheat germ, rye flour, and oats, plus enough bread flour to make a soft dough.
3. On a floured surface, knead dough about 10 minutes or until dough is smooth and elastic.
4. Place dough in a greased bowl; cover loosely with oiled plastic wrap. Let rise in warm place until doubled in size, about 30 minutes.
5. Punch down dough. Shape into 1 round loaf.
6. Place into a greased pie pan sprinkled with cornmeal. Cover with oiled plastic wrap and let rise until doubled in size (about 1 hour).
7. Brush with egg white and sprinkle with wheat germ, sunflower kernels, or oatmeal. Bake at 350° for 35 to 40 minutes.

Note: If bread is becoming too dark, cover loosely with foil the last 10 to 15 minutes of baking. Remove from pie pan and cool on a wire rack.

Cocoa Mix

1 cup non-dairy creamer
1 cup nonfat dry milk
$\frac{3}{4}$ cup sugar
$\frac{1}{2}$ cup unsweetened cocoa

1. Combine ingredients in a large bowl. Mix well.
2. Store in airtight containers.
3. To serve: place 2-3 heaping tablespoons in a mug. Add 1 cup boiling water and stir well. Garnish with miniature marshmallows or whipped cream, if desired.

North Dakota Dinner

1 lb ground beef
1 small onion, chopped
5 medium potatoes, peeled and sliced
2 tsp flour

2 T butter, melted
32 oz cream-style corn
1 tsp paprika

1. Preheat oven to 325°. Brown ground beef and onions. Drain. Put half of ground beef into casserole dish, then layer half of sliced potatoes; add remaining ground beef and then remaining potatoes.
2. Sprinkle flour over potatoes and drizzle with 1 T butter. Cover with creamed corn and sprinkle with paprika. Drizzle with remaining butter.
3. Bake, uncovered, for 1 hour or until potatoes are done.

Oatmeal Applesauce Cake

2¼ cups all-purpose flour
1 tsp salt
½ T baking soda
2 tsp baking powder
½ T cinnamon
½ tsp nutmeg

½ tsp ground cloves
1½ cups oats
⅓ cup oil
1¾ cups pure maple syrup
2 eggs plus 1 egg white
1½ cups unsweetened applesauce

1. Stir together all dry ingredients.
2. In a large bowl, blend oil and maple syrup with an electric mixer.
3. Add eggs and beat on high for 5 minutes. Blend in applesauce. Gradually add in the dry ingredients.
4. Pour batter into a Bundt pan that has been lightly coated with cooking spray. Bake at 350° for 45-55 minutes or until a knife inserted in the center comes out clean.
5. Invert onto a serving plate and remove pan immediately after removing cake from oven.

FOOD FACTS

- Dakota Bread was created to help celebrate 100 years of statehood.
- In 1893, Cream of Wheat was developed in Grand Forks.
- The largest hamburger was made in Rutland, North Dakota, in 1982. It weighed 3,591 pounds and fed almost 8,000 people.
- North Dakota grows more sunflowers than any other state.

Chicken Potpie

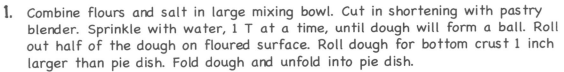

1½ cups whole wheat flour
½ cup white flour
1 tsp salt
¾ cup shortening
5 T cold water
1 cup chicken broth

cornstarch
2 cups chicken, cooked and chopped
16 oz frozen mixed vegetables
salt and pepper
1 egg white, beaten

1. Combine flours and salt in large mixing bowl. Cut in shortening with pastry blender. Sprinkle with water, 1 T at a time, until dough will form a ball. Roll out half of the dough on floured surface. Roll dough for bottom crust 1 inch larger than pie dish. Fold dough and unfold into pie dish.
2. Bake bottom crust at 425° for 10 minutes so that the crust will not be soggy.
3. Roll out other half of dough to form top crust. Bring chicken broth to a boil and thicken with a small amount of cornstarch to make gravy.
4. In large mixing bowl, combine gravy, chicken, and vegetables. Stir to coat, salt and pepper to taste, pour into pie shell, and top with crust. Brush top of pie crust with egg white, and bake at 425° for 30-35 minutes.

Cabbage and Barley Soup

¼ cup barley
4 cups chicken broth
5 T oil
4 cups chopped cabbage
2 onions, chopped

¼ cup fresh parsley
4 T flour
4 cups milk
4 chicken bouillon cubes
½ tsp celery salt
salt and pepper

1. Combine barley and chicken broth in a large stockpot. Cover and simmer for 2 hours.
2. Sauté onions, cabbage, and parsley in 3 T oil until soft, but do not brown.
3. Combine 2 T oil with flour, milk, chicken bouillon cubes, and celery salt. Cook until thickened and add to barley and broth.
4. Stir in sautéed cabbage and onion. Simmer for an additional 10-15 minutes to combine flavors. Salt and pepper to taste.

Buckeyes

We're not from Ohio, but these are a Christmas tradition at our house!

2 lbs peanut butter   1 lb butter
3 lbs powdered sugar   24 oz chocolate chips
½ bar paraffin wax

1. Mix peanut butter, butter, and sugar until dough forms.
2. Form into small balls and refrigerate 1 hour.
3. Melt chocolate and wax in double boiler.
4. Dip peanut butter balls in chocolate mixture ¾ of the way. Place on cookie sheets lined with waxed paper and refrigerate.

FOOD FACTS

- Ohio grows more tomatoes in hothouses than any other state.
- Tomato juice is the official state beverage.
- Good Humor Ice Cream was started in Youngstown in 1920.
- Ohio native Harry M. Stevens created the first dining dog when he introduced America to the ever popular hot dog in 1900.
- Ohio's key agricultural products are soybeans, dairy products, corn, tomatoes, hogs, cattle, poultry, and eggs.

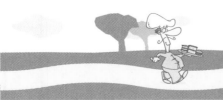

Chili

1 lb ground beef	2 tsp chili powder
1 medium onion, chopped	1/2 tsp ground cumin
1 15-oz can pinto beans, rinsed and drained	1/2 tsp salt
2 16-oz cans peeled tomatoes	1/2 tsp ground black pepper
1/2 cup water	1/4 cup fresh cilantro, chopped

1. In a nonstick skillet, sauté the ground beef and onion until meat is browned and onion is tender.
2. Add the pinto beans, tomatoes, water, and seasonings.
3. Cover and simmer for 1 hour, adding more water if chili becomes too thick.
4. Add chopped cilantro and simmer an additional 10 minutes.

Spoon Bread

2 eggs, beaten	1 can whole kernel corn, drained
8 1/2-oz package corn muffin mix	8 oz sour cream
1 can creamed corn	1 stick butter, melted

1. Combine all ingredients.
2. Pour into baking dish lightly coated with cooking spray.
3. Bake at 350° for 35-40 minutes or until golden brown.

Caramel Cake

This recipe brings back fond memories of childhood cookouts during our years living near the Texas/Oklahoma state line.

2 sticks butter, softened
3 cups sugar
6 eggs
1 tsp salt

$2^2/_3$ cups all-purpose flour
$^1/_4$ tsp baking soda
1 cup sour cream
1 T vanilla

1. Cream butter and sugar until fluffy.
2. Add eggs, 1 at a time.
3. Sift together dry ingredients. Add alternately with sour cream to butter mixture. Add vanilla.
4. Pour into 1 9x13-inch or 3 round cake pans that have been greased and floured.
5. Bake at 325° for 25 to 35 minutes. Test for doneness.
6. Cool for 10 minutes; remove from pan; cool completely. Frost.

Frosting:

2 sticks butter
$^1/_2$ tsp vanilla
2 cups light brown sugar
4 cups powdered sugar
$^1/_2$ cup evaporated milk

1. Melt butter.
2. Add brown sugar and milk. Cook over medium heat 2 minutes, stirring constantly. Remove from heat.
3. Add vanilla.
4. Pour over powdered sugar and beat until smooth.
5. Cool slightly and frost cake.

FOOD FACTS

- The official state meal of Oklahoma includes fried okra, squash, cornbread, barbecue pork, sausage and gravy, grits, corn, strawberries, chicken-fried steak, and black-eyed peas.
- Okmulgee, Oklahoma, holds the world's record for largest pecan pie, pecan cookie, and pecan brownie.
- The world's largest McDonald's, on I-44 at Vinita, Oklahoma, is actually built over the highway, with entrances on both sides.

Apple-Glazed Beef Brisket

4-5 lbs boneless beef brisket
1 medium onion, quartered
2 large garlic cloves, halved
10 whole cloves
water
10 oz apple jelly

3 T Dijon-style mustard
3 T chopped green onion
1½ tsp salt
¾ tsp cracked black peppercorns
¾ tsp curry powder
parsley

1. Place brisket, onion, garlic, and cloves in large Dutch oven. Add water to cover. Bring to a boil, reduce heat, cover, and simmer 2½-3 hours or until tender. Drain brisket, cover, and refrigerate up to 24 hours.
2. Combine apple jelly, mustard, green onions, salt, pepper, and curry powder in small saucepan and heat until jelly melts, stirring occasionally.
3. Place brisket in shallow roasting pan; brush with glaze. Roast at 325° for 45 minutes, basting frequently with glaze. Carve brisket into thin slices and serve with remaining glaze; garnish with parsley.

Zesty Hazelnut Broccoli

1 large clove garlic, minced
1 T oil
1 bunch (1½ lbs) broccoli, chopped
¼ cup water
½ cup sour cream

1 tsp horseradish
¼ tsp thyme
½ tsp marjoram
salt and pepper to taste
½ cup roasted and chopped hazelnuts

1. Sauté garlic in oil. Add broccoli and water. Cover and steam until tender crisp over medium heat. (Most of the liquid should be gone.)
3. Add sour cream and seasonings.
4. Heat until sauce slightly thickens.
5. Add nuts, toss, and serve.

Blackberry Pie

1 cup sugar

3 T all-purpose flour

pinch of salt

4 cups fresh blackberries

pie crust

2 T butter

1 T sugar

1. Combine 1 cup sugar, flour, and salt in a large bowl. Add blackberries and toss.
2. Pour into bottom pie crust. Dot with butter.
3. Top with remaining pie crust. Fold and crimp edges. Cut slits in top. Sprinkle with 1 T sugar. Loosely tent edge with thin strips of foil to prevent over-browning.
4. Bake at 400° for 40 minutes.

FUN FACTS

- The Pacific golden chanterelle is the official state mushroom.
- The hazelnut, or filbert, is the official state nut.
- Oregon is the nation's top producer of pears, blackberries, and hazelnuts.

Pennsylvania

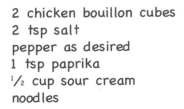

These recipes come from my mother-in-law's family in Allentown.

Chicken Paprika

2½ to 3 pounds chicken pieces
⅓ cup flour
oil
2 onions, thinly sliced
1½ cups water

2 chicken bouillon cubes
2 tsp salt
pepper as desired
1 tsp paprika
½ cup sour cream
noodles

1. Coat chicken with flour; reserve remaining flour. Brown chicken in hot oil, remove from pan.
2. Cook onions and remaining flour in hot oil for 2-3 minutes. Stir in water, bouillon, salt, pepper, and paprika.
3. Return chicken to pan, cover and simmer for 30-40 minutes.
4. Stir in sour cream; serve with noodles.

Carrot Fritters

1 lb carrots, peeled and chopped
¼ cup onion, chopped fine
½ cup water
2 eggs
½ cup flour

¼ tsp salt
⅛ tsp paprika
1 T dry parsley
oil
mustard for dipping, if desired

1. Combine carrots with onion and water in a saucepan. Bring to a boil, then simmer covered until carrots are tender. Drain liquid into a measuring cup. Measure ½ cup of liquid into a small bowl.
2. Separate eggs. Set aside the whites in another small bowl.
3. Add the yolks to the reserved liquid and mix. Add flour, salt, and paprika and beat until smooth. Stir in carrots and onions.
4. Beat egg whites until stiff but not dry. Fold into carrot mixture.
5. Heat some oil for frying in a griddle or skillet. Drop batter by heaping table-spoonful and fry until golden brown, both sides.

Pumpkin Nut Cake

2 cups canned pumpkin
1¼ cup oil
4 eggs
2 cups sugar
1 tsp salt

2 cups all-purpose flour
2 tsp cinnamon
2 tsp baking soda
1 tsp baking powder
½ cup chopped nuts

1. Beat together all ingredients except nuts. Add nuts.
2. Pour into 9x13-inch pan.
3. Bake at 350° for 45-50 minutes.

Frosting

4 T butter
2½ cups powdered sugar
8 oz cream cheese
1 tsp vanilla

1. Beat all ingredients together until smooth.
2. Spread over cake.

FOOD FACTS

- Hershey, Pennsylvania, is home to the world's largest chocolate factory.
- Philadelphia is famous for its Philly Cheesesteak sandwiches.
- Ice cream soda was invented in Philadelphia in 1874 by Robert Green.
- In Hazleton, Pennsylvania, it is illegal to drink a carbonated beverage while lecturing in a school auditorium.
- The chocolate chip cookie is the official state cookie.
- Funnel cakes, a deep-fried pastry made by pouring the batter through a funnel into hot fat and then coating with powdered sugar, are a Pennsylvania Dutch specialty.

Rhode Island

Rhode Island Red Clam Chowder

¼ cup bacon, finely cut up
¼ cup finely chopped onion
2 (8-oz) cans minced or whole clams
2 cups potatoes, peeled and finely chopped
1 cup water
⅓ cup chopped celery
1 (16-oz) can whole tomatoes, undrained
2 tsp fresh chopped parsley
1 tsp salt
¼ tsp dried thyme
⅛ tsp pepper

1. In large kettle, cook bacon and onion until bacon is crisp and onion is tender.
2. Drain clams and reserve liquid.
3. To bacon and onion, add clam liquid, potatoes, water, and celery. Cook about 10 minutes, until potatoes are tender.
4. Add clams, tomatoes, parsley, salt, thyme, and pepper.
5. Heat to boiling, stirring occasionally.

Mocha Cake

⅔ cup Dutch cocoa
1⅓ cups hot water, divided
6 T instant coffee granules, divided
2 sticks butter, softened
1¾ cups sugar
3 large eggs

2 tsp vanilla
2¼ cups all-purpose flour
1¼ tsp baking soda
¼ tsp baking powder
¼ tsp salt

1. Stir together cocoa, ⅔ cup hot water, and 3 T coffee granules until smooth. Cool.
2. Stir together remaining ⅔ cup hot water and remaining 3 T coffee granules; cool.
3. Beat cocoa mixture, butter, sugar, eggs, and vanilla at medium speed with an electric mixer until blended.
4. Stir together flour, baking soda, baking powder, and salt; add to butter mixture alternately with remaining coffee granules, beating at low speed and beginning and ending with flour mixture. Beat 1 minute.
5. Pour into 2 greased and floured 9-inch round cake pans. Bake at 325° for 30-35 minutes or until a wooden pick inserted in center comes out clean.
6. Cool in pans on wire racks for 10 minutes; remove from pans, and cool completely on wire racks.

Mocha Frosting:

2 sticks butter, softened
1 cup Dutch cocoa
¼ tsp salt
½ cup coffee liqueur

2 lbs powdered sugar
¼ cup strong brewed coffee, cooled
¼ cup whipping cream

1. Beat butter at medium speed until creamy.
2. Gradually add cocoa and salt alternately with liqueur, beating until blended.
3. Gradually add powdered sugar alternately with coffee and whipping cream, beating until blended.

FOOD FACTS

- One tuna caught off the coast of Rhode Island can weigh half a ton!
- Rhode Island is the only place in the world where you can get coffee milk. Coffee milk is simply milk mixed with coffee syrup. In 1993 a contest took place that pitted coffee milk against Del's Lemonade to see which one would reign supreme as Little Rhody's top beverage. Coffee milk won out, and the Rhode Island Legislature pronounced it the state's official drink.
- Coffee milk isn't the only coffee-based product that Rhode Islanders enjoy; they also purchase an inordinate amount of other hot and cold coffee beverages, coffee ice cream, and even coffee-flavored gelatin.

South Carolina

This meal would be typical in the upstate of South Carolina.

Savory Baked Bird

1 chicken, cut up
salt and pepper
meat tenderizer
Cajun seasoning
1/4 cup + 2 T teriyaki sauce
1 lemon

1 onion, sliced
flour
1 T parsley flakes
1/2–1 cup chicken broth
1 T breadcrumbs
1 T Parmesan cheese

1. Season chicken with salt, pepper, meat tenderizer, and Cajun seasoning (Tony Chachere's, if possible). Place in a glass casserole dish.
2. Pour teriyaki sauce and the juice from 1 lemon over chicken. Top with sliced onion and parsley. Refrigerate at least 6 hours. Pour off marinade; reserve.
3. Lightly flour chicken and return to casserole dish lightly coated with cooking spray.
4. Pour marinade over chicken. Pour chicken broth around sides of casserole dish. Sprinkle with breadcrumbs and Parmesan cheese. Top with reserved onion.
5. Bake, covered, at 400° for 1–1½ hours.

Dilled Squash Bread

1 cup Bisquick
1/2 cup Parmesan cheese
1 T dill weed
1 tsp salt
1/8 tsp pepper

1 T onion powder
4 eggs, beaten
1/2 cup oil
2 cups chopped zucchini
2 cups chopped yellow squash

1. Combine dry ingredients.
2. Add oil and eggs, mix well.
3. Stir in zucchini and squash.
4. Bake, uncovered, at 375° for 30 minutes or until done.

90

Fudge Ribbon Cake

1 chocolate fudge cake mix
8 oz cream cheese
2 T butter
1 T cornstarch

14 oz sweetened condensed milk
1 egg
1 tsp vanilla

1. Prepare cake mix as directed.
2. Pour into greased and floured 10-inch tube pan.
3. In small bowl, beat cream cheese, butter, and cornstarch until fluffy.
4. Gradually add condensed milk, egg, and vanilla. Pour evenly over batter.
5. Bake at 350° for 1 hour. Cool completely.

Frosting

½ cup butter
3 T cocoa
⅓ cup milk

1 lb powdered sugar
1 cup chopped pecans
1 tsp vanilla

1. Combine butter, cocoa, and milk and bring to a boil.
2. Remove from heat and add sugar, nuts, and vanilla.
3. Cool slightly and frost cake. Refrigerate.

FOOD FACTS

- South Carolina's first cash crop was rice, which grew well in the swampy areas along the coast.
- The United States' first tea plantation was near Charleston.
- South Carolina is the top grower of peaches in the country.
- St. George, South Carolina, eats more pounds of grits per capita than anywhere else in the world.
- The official state fruit is the peach.

South Dakota

Ham and Broccoli Casserole

10 oz frozen, chopped broccoli
12 slices white bread, crusts removed
2 cups diced ham
2 T finely chopped onion
1 cup shredded cheddar cheese

6 eggs, slightly beaten
3 1/2 cups milk
1/2 tsp salt
1/2 tsp dry mustard

1. Grease a 9x13-inch pan.
2. Partially cook broccoli; drain well.
3. Cut off crusts and cube bread; spread in pan.
4. Layer ham, then broccoli. Sprinkle onion, then cheese.
5. In large bowl, combine beaten eggs, milk, salt, and mustard. Pour over bread.
6. Cover; refrigerate 6 hours or overnight.
7. Bake uncovered at 325 ° for 1 1/4 hours until inserted knife comes out clean. Let stand 10 minutes before serving.

Kuchen

An official state recipe

For the crust:
2 cups flour
$\frac{1}{2}$ cup sugar
$\frac{1}{4}$ tsp kosher salt

$\frac{1}{2}$ tsp vanilla extract
$\frac{1}{2}$ lb (2 sticks) unsalted butter, cold and cut into pieces

For the filling:
1 pound cream cheese, at room temperature
$\frac{3}{4}$ cup sugar

1 tsp vanilla extract
1 egg, at room temperature

For the topping:
2 T sugar
$1\frac{1}{2}$ tsp ground cinnamon

3 Granny Smith apples, peeled, cored, and thinly sliced

1. Preheat the oven to 450°.
2. Lightly grease and flour a 9x13-inch pan.
3. Place the flour, sugar, and salt in a large bowl or food processor fitted with a steel blade and mix to combine.
4. Add the vanilla and butter, a little at a time. Press into the baking pan and bake in oven until slightly golden but not brown, about 12 to 15 minutes. Cool.
5. Lower the oven temperature to 400°.

To make the filling and topping:
1. Mix the cream cheese, sugar, and vanilla in mixer and beat until creamy.
2. Add the egg, mix to combine, and pour over the cooled crust.
3. Place the sugar and cinnamon in a small bowl and mix to combine.
4. Place the apples on top of the filling in 2 or 3 columns.
5. Sprinkle with the cinnamon sugar.
6. Bake until firm and a rich brown, about 20 minutes.

FOOD FACTS
- Kuchen is South Dakota's official state dessert.
- South Dakota's main agricultural products are cattle, soybeans, corn, wheat, and hogs.

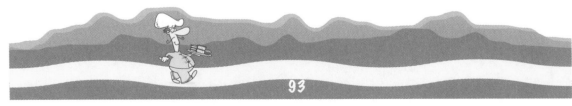

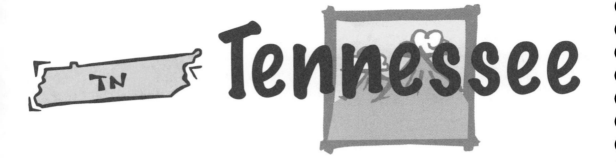

Tennessee

Hoppin' John

1 cup black-eyed peas
5-6 cups water
hot pepper sauce, to taste

1 smoked ham hock
1 medium onion, chopped
salt
1 cup long-grain white rice

1. Wash and sort the peas. Place them in a saucepan with water.
2. Add pepper sauce, ham hock, onion, and salt to taste.
3. Gently boil, uncovered, until peas are tender but not mushy (about 1½ hours or until 2 cups of liquid remain).
4. Add the rice to the pot, cover, and simmer over low heat for about 20 minutes, never lifting the lid.
5. Remove from heat and allow to steam, still covered, for another 10 minutes.

Corn Salad

1 quart frozen shoepeg corn, cooked, drained
1 bell pepper, seeded, chopped
1 cup sliced cherry tomatoes
½ cup chopped purple onion
¾ cup chopped cucumber
½ cup mayonnaise

¼ cup sour cream
1 T apple cider vinegar
½ tsp celery salt
½ tsp white pepper
salt to taste

1. Combine all ingredients in a large bowl and mix gently.
2. Chill, covered, for 3 hours or longer.

Butterscotch Pecan Cream Cheese Pound Cake

1 cup butter
8 oz cream cheese, softened
2¼ cups sugar
6 large eggs
2 tsp vanilla
1 tsp butter flavoring
1 tsp nut flavoring
2⅔ cup all-purpose flour
1 cup chopped pecans, toasted
⅔ cup butterscotch chips

1. Beat butter and cream cheese for 2 minutes at medium speed. Gradually add sugar. Add eggs 1 at a time, beating after each addition just until yellow disappears. Add flavorings.
2. Gradually add flour at lowest speed just until blended. Stir in pecans and butterscotch chips. Spoon batter into greased and floured bundt pan.
3. Bake at 325° 1 hour and 20 minutes or until toothpick inserted in middle comes out clean. Cool for 10 minutes. Remove from pan and cool completely.

FOOD FACTS

- Coca-Cola was first bottled in 1899 in Chattanooga.
- In 1932, Herman Lay started a potato chip company in Nashville. In 1961, the company merged with the Frito Company and became known as Frito-Lay.
- Clarence Saunders of Memphis started the world's first supermarket. The name of the store was Piggly Wiggly.

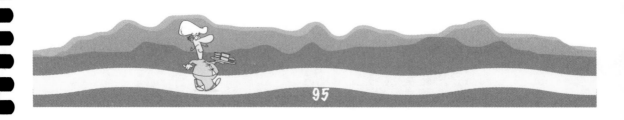

Chicken Fried Steak with Milk Gravy

1 sleeve saltine crackers, crushed
1¼ cups flour
½ tsp baking powder
2 tsp salt
¼ tsp ground red pepper

1½ tsp black pepper
1 lb cube steaks
2 eggs
4¾ cups milk
oil

1. Combine cracker crumbs, 1 cup flour, baking powder, 1 tsp salt, red pepper, and ½ tsp black pepper. Season steaks with salt and pepper.
2. Beat eggs with ¾ cup milk. Coat steaks with cracker mixture. Dip in egg mixture. Coat again with cracker mixture. Fry in hot oil until golden brown.
3. Drain oil, reserving cracklings and 1 T oil in pan.
4. Whisk 4 cups milk, ¼ cup flour, 1 tsp salt, and 1 tsp pepper together. Whisk into reserved oil and cracklings. Whisk constantly until thick and bubbly. Serve with mashed potatoes.

Texas Ranger Soup

1 lb 9-or 15-bean soup beans
10-oz can Rotel tomatoes and green chilis
1 lb ham, diced
16-oz can diced tomatoes and liquid
1 large onion, chopped
salt and pepper to taste
1 clove garlic, chopped

1. Wash and sort beans.
2. Place in a stockpot and cover with water 2 inches above beans. Let soak overnight. Drain beans.
3. Cover with water and add the other ingredients.
4. Bring to a boil; reduce heat and simmer, covered, for about 2 hours until the beans are done. Stir occasionally to prevent sticking. Add a little bit of water, if necessary, to prevent sticking.

Pecan Pie

3 eggs
dash salt
⅓ cup butter
single pie crust

⅔ cup sugar
1 cup light corn syrup
1 cup pecan halves

May be mixed by hand or with an electric mixer.
1. Beat eggs.
2. Add sugar and salt; mix until dissolved.
3. Stir in corn syrup and melted butter; mix well. Stir in pecans.
4. Pour into unbaked pie shell.
5. Cover edges with narrow strips of foil to prevent burning.
6. Bake at 350° for 50 minutes or until knife inserted in middle comes out clean. Remove foil during last 10 minutes of baking, if desired.

FOOD FACTS
- Texas raises more beef cattle than any other state.
- Texas is also the leading grower of blue corn.
- Theme park Six Flags over Texas is home to a popular cherry-flavored frozen confection called Pink Things.
- The Texas Red Grapefruit is the state fruit.
- Texas has 2 official peppers, the jalapeno and the chiltepin.
- Chili is the official state dish.
- The official state vegetable is the Texas Sweet onion.
- Dr Pepper was invented in Waco, Texas, in 1885.

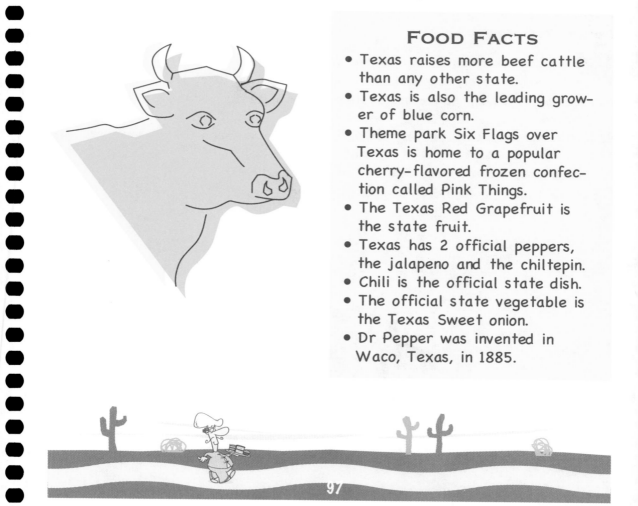

Utah Steak and Beans

1 cup dried beans
1½ T oil
1½ pounds chuck steak,
   cut in bite-sized pieces
1 onion, chopped

1 T honey
1 tsp salt
¼ tsp pepper
¾ tsp prepared mustard

1. Soak beans overnight in enough water to cover.
2. In the same water, simmer beans 20 minutes. Drain beans, reserving water.
3. Heat oil in a large saucepan. Sauté onion until tender. Add meat; cook until browned.
4. Combine honey, salt, pepper, mustard, and reserved bean water. Add more water if necessary to total 1½ cups.
5. Add beans to meat; mix well. Stir in liquid.
6. Cover; simmer 3 hours, until meat is tender.

Cinnamon Pull-Apart Bread

1 packet yeast
1 cup lukewarm water or milk
1 cup wheat flour
1 T wheat germ
1 tsp salt
3 T oil

3 T honey
2 cups bread flour
¼ cup butter, melted
¼ cup cinnamon
½ cup sugar

1. Turn on the oven for a few minutes and then turn it off.
2. Mix the yeast with the warm water. Stir in the wheat flour, wheat germ, salt, olive oil, and honey. Add the bread flour until it is difficult to stir.
3. Oil your fingers and mix the remaining flour with your hands. The dough should form a ball and pull away from the sides of the bowl.
4. Grease or spray a pan with nonstick spray.
5. Melt the butter.
6. Mix the cinnamon and sugar in another bowl.
7. Cut the dough into 1-inch balls with kitchen shears. Roll the dough balls in butter then in cinnamon sugar. Place in pan.
8. Cover the pan with towel and set it in a warm, draft-free place (the oven) to rise for 1-2 hours until it has doubled in size.
9. Bake at 350° for 20-25 minutes.

NOTE: This dough recipe also works well in a bread machine or a mixer with a dough hook.

FOOD FACTS

- The cherry is the official state fruit.
- The residents of Salt Lake City eat more lime-flavored gelatin than any other city in the U.S.
- The people of Utah love candy. In fact, they eat twice as much candy per person as any other state.

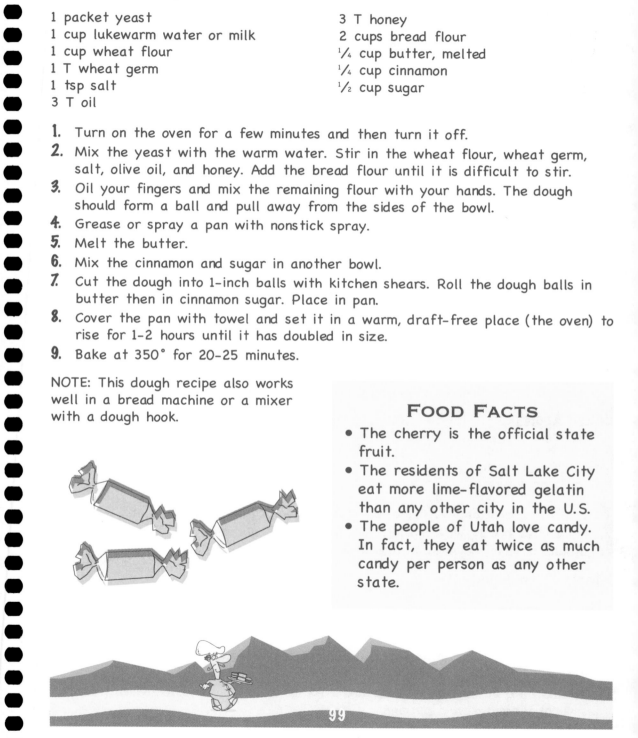

Vermont

Roast Turkey and Stuffing

1 10-lb turkey
10-12 slices dried bread, crumbled
2 tsp celery salt
1 tsp nutmeg
4 T chopped parsley
salt and pepper to taste

1/4 tsp ground mace
2 tsp chopped pecans
3 hard-boiled eggs, chopped
1 1/2 cup chopped mushrooms
1 large onion, chopped fine
1 stick butter
2 cups chicken broth

1. Season turkey with black pepper, garlic powder, and paprika on both sides to taste.
2. Place breast down in roasting pan. Add 2 cups of water to bottom of pan. Bake, covered, at 200° for 6-7 hours.

Stuffing:
1. Combine breadcrumbs, seasonings, pecans, and eggs in a large bowl.
2. Saute mushrooms and onion in butter; combine with bread mixture, moisten with chicken broth. Spoon into baking dish. Bake, covered, at 325° for 30-45 minutes.

Baked Apples

4 large baking apples
1/4 cup brown sugar
2 T nuts or raisins

1/4 tsp cinnamon
2 T butter
1/4 cup water

1. Wash and core apples. Combine sugar, nuts or raisins, cinnamon, and butter.
2. Fill apples evenly with mixture. Place in microwave-safe dish. Pour water around bottom. Cover with plastic wrap. Microwave on high 7-8 minutes.

Maple-Coated Walnuts

3 cups whole walnuts
1/2 cup dark or extra dark maple syrup

1/4 cup water

1. Combine ingredients in heavy saucepan. Simmer over low heat until nuts have absorbed the syrup, stirring continually.
2. Spread on greased cookie sheet and bake at 325 for about 10 minutes. Stir several times to avoid burning.

Vermont Maple Candy

Pure Maple Syrup (Grade A Light Amber or Medium Amber works best.) Amount depends on how much candy you want to make. A quart (4 cups) will make 2 pounds of candy.

A few drops of butter or vegetable oil.

1. Fill deep pot or pan partially with water and candy thermometer. Bring to a boil, and note the temperature of the boiling water. (Since water boils at different temperatures in different locations—depending on air pressure, it is important to follow this step).

2. Empty the pan. Place syrup in deep pan, as the syrup will foam up fairly high when boiling. Add a few drops of oil or butter. (This helps to keep foam down). Also, buttering the rim can be an effective technique for keeping foam down.

3. Boil carefully over high heat without stirring, until temperature of the boiling syrup is 28° above the boiling point of the water. Watch carefully as the temperature climbs higher. It can get too hot very quickly near the end. If your pan boils over, you'll have a real mess! If it cooks too long it can scorch, or even catch fire. Watch it! (This is not a place for small children, as the boiling syrup is VERY hot and can stick and burn). Remove from heat, and let cool for 3-5 minutes.

4. Stir evenly (don't beat) until the liquid loses its gloss and starts to become opaque. This should take a few minutes. The tricky part is to learn the exact correct moment to pour off.
Stir too long and the thickened syrup will "set up" (harden) in the pan. If this happens, add a cup of water, and reheat slowly to dissolve sugar, then start over. If you don't stir long enough, the sugar may not "set up" in the molds at all.

5. Pour carefully into rubber molds. Small aluminum foil pans can be used. Allow to cool, remove from molds, and place on a rack to dry for a few hours.

FOOD FACTS

- Ten gallons of sap are needed to produce 1 quart of maple syrup.
- Vermont produces more maple syrup than any other state in the U.S.
- Montpelier, Vermont, is the only U.S. state capital without a McDonald's restaurant.
- In 1978, Ben and Jerry's ice cream was started in Burlington, Vermont, in a renovated gas station.

Virginia

Ham with Ham Gravy

This is my great-grandmother's ham gravy recipe. It was passed down orally until 1988, when my mother wrote it down.

1. Place shank portion ham in a large roasting pan, fat side up. Pour in 1-2 cups of water, depending on the size of the ham.
2. Bake, covered, at 200° for 6-8 hours. Serve with gravy and mashed potatoes.

Gravy:

Juice from ham
1 cup chopped bell pepper
1 cup chopped onion
1 cup chopped celery
1 can diced tomatoes
1 T mustard
cornstarch

1. Combine ham broth and vegetables in a saucepan or skillet.
2. Bring to a boil and cook until tender. Stir in mustard.
3. Thicken with cornstarch mixed with water.

Turnip Greens

Another of Nanny's specialties. Uncle Rich helped me with the measurements and instructions.

1 quart water
¼ lb ham chunks or ¼ lb salt pork
1 bunch turnip greens with root
¼ cup oil
½ T sugar
salt to taste with ham chunks (do not add salt with salt pork)

1. In a large pot bring water to a boil; add meat, reduce heat, and simmer until tender.
2. Wash greens and peel turnip roots. Cut the turnips and the roots to desired size.
3. Add oil, turnips, roots, sugar, and salt to pot and bring to a boil.
4. Reduce heat and simmer for about 30-45 minutes or until turnips and roots are tender.

Pea-Picking Cake

This is my mother's favorite cake. The recipe came from her sister, my Aunt Flaudie.

1 yellow cake mix
1 11-oz can mandarin oranges in juice
4 eggs
½ cup oil

1. Beat all ingredients until well blended.
2. Pour batter into 3 greased and floured round cake pans.
3. Bake at 350° for 25 minutes. Cool completely.

Topping:

1 20-oz can crushed pineapple in juice   1 16-oz tub non-dairy whipped topping
1 3.4-oz box vanilla pudding

1. Combine pineapple and pudding.
2. Fold in whipped topping.
3. Spread in between layers and on top of cake.

FOOD FACTS

- Virginia is known for its ham. England's Queen Victoria liked them so well that she had a standing order for 6 per week.
- "Genuine Smithfield hams [are those] cut from the carcasses of peanut-fed hogs, raised in the peanut-belt of the State of Virginia or the State of North Carolina, and which are cured, treated, smoked, and processed in the town of Smithfield, in the State of Virginia" (1926 Statute passed by General Assembly of Virginia).
- Before Thomas Jefferson bit into a tomato and found it to be edible, people thought that tomatoes were poisonous.
- Thomas Jefferson is also credited with introducing our country to a favorite treat-ice cream.
- The first known recipe for ketchup comes from an 1824 Virginia cookbook.
- The first peanuts grown in the United States were grown in Virginia.

103

Washington

Baked Potato Soup

4 large potatoes
²/₃ cup butter
²/₃ cup flour
6 cups milk
salt and pepper

4 green onions, sliced
1 cup sour cream
2 cups crisp-cooked, crumbled bacon
¹/₂ cup grated cheddar cheese

1. Bake potatoes.
2. Melt butter in a medium saucepan. Slowly blend in flour with a wire whisk until thoroughly blended. Gradually add in milk, whisking constantly. Simmer over low heat, stirring constantly. Stir in salt and pepper.
3. Cut potatoes in half, scoop out, and set aside. Chop half the potato peels and discard the remainder.
4. When milk mixture is very hot, whisk in potato. Add green onion and chopped potato peels; whisk well. Add sour cream and crumbled bacon. Heat thoroughly. Add cheese, a little at a time, until melted.

Apple Dumplings

pastry for 9-inch pie
6 apples, peeled and cored
1 cup sugar
2 cups water
4 T butter
½ tsp cinnamon

1. Preheat oven to 425°.
2. Roll pastry to less than ⅛-inch thickness. Cut into 6 squares.
3. Combine sugar, water, 3 T butter, and cinnamon in saucepan. Boil 30 minutes.
4. Place 1 apple on each square of pastry. Fill cavities with cinnamon and sugar (not the syrup). Top with butter.
6. Bring opposite points of pastry over apple. Moisten with water to seal.
7. Lift gently and place in baking dish. Do not allow dumplings to touch.
8. Pour syrup over dumplings. Bake 40-45 minutes or until golden brown. Occasionally spoon syrup over dumplings during baking.

Serve hot or cold with ice cream or whipped cream.

FOOD FACTS

- The apple is the official state fruit.
- Washington grows more apples than any other state.
- Washington grows a very sweet onion called the Walla Walla. The onion was named for the valley where it is grown.

West Virginia

I had to prepare both of these in order to figure out the measurements to these old family recipes.

Fried Chicken

1 quart buttermilk
1 chicken, cut up
1 tsp salt

1 tsp pepper
1 cup flour
oil

1. Soak chicken in buttermilk for 6-8 hours in the refrigerator.
2. Drain and rinse chicken.
3. Season chicken with ½ tsp salt and ½ tsp pepper.
4. Combine flour, ½ tsp salt, and ½ tsp pepper.
5. Dredge chicken in flour mixture.
6. Fry in hot oil, covered or uncovered. Drain on paper towels.

Fried Okra

1 lb fresh okra, sliced
½-¾ cup cornmeal
½ tsp salt

¼ tsp pepper
oil

1. Place okra in a bowl and cover with water. Drain (okra needs to be very damp for cornmeal to stick).
2. Combine cornmeal, salt, and pepper. Coat okra with cornmeal mixture.
3. Fry, in batches, in hot oil until golden brown. Drain on paper towels.

Banana Bread

¼ cup butter, melted
3 ripe bananas, mashed
1½ cups self-rising flour

1 cup sugar
1 egg
½ cup chopped nuts

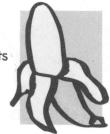

1. Combine ingredients until well blended.
2. Pour into a buttered bread pan.
3. Bake at 350° for 1 hour.

Hot Applesauce Crispy

1 cup Bisquick
½ cup sugar
½ cup brown sugar
¼ cup butter, softened

16 oz applesauce
½ cup chopped walnuts or pecans
½ tsp cinnamon
¼ tsp nutmeg

1. Combine Bisquick and sugars. Cut in butter with a fork or pastry blender until crumbly; set aside.
2. Combine remaining ingredients and pour into an 8-inch pan.
3. Sprinkle crumb mixture over applesauce mixture.
4. Bake at 400° for 20 minutes.

FOOD FACTS

- Golden Delicious apples were first grown in Clay County, West Virginia.
- The apple is the official state fruit.
- A law in West Virginia allows residents to eat road kill. If you run over an animal, you can legally take it home and cook it for dinner as long as you report it within 12 hours.

Cheesy Garlic Rolls

up to 5½ cups flour, divided
3 T sugar
2 tsp salt
1 package active dry yeast (¼ oz)
1½ cups milk
½ cup water

½ cup butter (1 stick)
2 T olive oil
2 tsp minced garlic
2 tsp dried chives
1 tsp dried Italian seasoning
⅔ cup sharp cheddar cheese, grated

1. Combine 3 cups flour, sugar, salt, and yeast in a large bowl. Combine milk and ½ cup water in saucepan; heat to 120°. Gradually stir milk mixture into flour mixture.

2. Stir in ¼ cup melted butter. Beat at low speed with electric mixer about 30 seconds, then beat at high for 1 minute. Gradually stir in enough of the remaining flour to make a soft dough.

3. Turn dough onto floured surface. Knead until smooth, 6-8 minutes. Place dough in a large bowl, cover, and let rise in a warm place for about 1 hour until double in bulk. Punch down dough, cover, and let rest 10 minutes.

4. Combine ¼ cup butter, olive oil, garlic, chives, and Italian seasoning in a bowl.

5. Divide dough into 24 pieces. Place a heaping tsp of grated cheddar in center of each dough piece and roll into a ball. Dip the balls in butter mixture and place in muffin tin. Drizzle remaining butter mixture over dough balls.

6. Cover and let rise in a warm place until double in bulk, about 45 minutes. Bake at 375° until golden brown, about 14 minutes.

Ribs with Sauerkraut and Potatoes

3-4 lbs country-style pork ribs
oil
2 27-oz cans sauerkraut

salt and pepper to taste
6-8 medium potatoes
1 stick butter

1. In large pot over medium heat, brown ribs in a small amount of oil. When ribs are browned, add sauerkraut, salt, and pepper.
2. Fill 1 sauerkraut can with water and add to meat. Cook covered over low heat until meat falls off the bones, 1 to 1½ hours, stirring occasionally. Remove bones.
3. Quarter potatoes and place in pot. Add butter. Cover and cook until potatoes are soft, about 45 minutes, stirring occasionally.

Carrot Cake

2 cups self-rising flour
2 cups sugar
1 tsp baking soda
2 tsp cinnamon
1 cup oil
4 eggs
3 cups grated carrot

Frosting:
1 stick butter, softened
8 oz cream cheese, softened
1 tsp vanilla
1 lb powdered sugar
1 cup pecans, finely chopped

Cream together butter and cream cheese. Add vanilla and powdered sugar; beat well. Stir in pecans.

1. Stir all dry ingredients together. Add oil and mix well. Add eggs and beat well. Stir in carrots.
2. Pour into 3 greased and floured 9-inch round pans. Bake at 300° for 20 minutes. Cakes are done when toothpick inserted in middle comes out clean.

*HINT For a moist cake: Bake cake a day ahead. Remove cake from pans onto individual plates that have been covered with wax paper. Once the layers are completely cool, wrap with plastic wrap and put in freezer. Frost the cake while it is frozen.

FOOD FACTS

- Wisconsin grows more carrots, peas, and sweet corn than any other state.
- Wisconsin is also the country's leading producer of milk and milk products.
- Malted milk and the ice cream sundae were both created in Wisconsin.

Wyoming

Cowboy Beans

10 slices bacon, browned and drained
1½ lb. ground beef
½ cup onion
⅓ cup brown sugar, packed
⅓ cup sugar
¼ cup ketchup
¼ cup barbecue sauce

2 T molasses
½ tsp salt
½ tsp chili powder
½ tsp pepper
2 T mustard
3 16-oz cans pork and beans

1. Brown ground beef and onion; drain. Combine with remaining ingredients.
2. Pour into baking dish. Bake at 350° for 1 hour.

Cornbread Cakes

1 cup cornmeal
1 cup flour
¼ cup sugar
4 tsp baking powder

¾ tsp salt
2 eggs
1½ cups milk
¼ cup oil

1. Combine dry ingredients.
2. Add remaining ingredients; mix well.
3. Pour batter ¼ cup at a time onto hot griddle coated with cooking spray or hot oil. Flip when edges are golden brown. Serve hot with butter.

Sheet Cake

1 cup butter, softened
2 cups sugar
3 cups cake flour
3 tsp baking powder
½ tsp salt

4 eggs
1 cup milk
1 tsp vanilla
½ tsp almond extract

1. Cream butter. Gradually add sugar, creaming until light and fluffy.
2. Add eggs 1 at a time, beating after each addition.
3. Combine dry ingredients. Add to creamed mixture alternately with milk and flavorings, beating after each addition until smooth.
4. Pour into greased 9x13-inch pan. Bake at 350° for 25-30 minutes or until done. Cool completely.

Frosting:

1 cup sugar
4 T cocoa
½ cup evaporated milk

1 tsp vanilla
2 T butter

1. Combine sugar, cocoa, milk, and vanilla in a saucepan.
2. Bring to a boil over medium heat. Cook for 1½ minutes, stirring constantly.
3. Remove from heat. Add butter and beat with a spoon until smooth.

FOOD FACTS

- On a cattle drive, the cook earned twice as much money as the cowboy.
- There wasn't much variety on a cattle drive. Most meals consisted of meat (when available), beans, cornbread cakes or sourdough biscuits, white gravy, and coffee.

Washington, D.C.

Red, White, and Blue Toast

A Pettit family Fourth of July breakfast tradition.

bread
cream cheese
blueberries
strawberry or raspberry jam

1. Toast bread.
2. Spread with cream cheese.
3. Arrange blueberries in a square in the upper left corner. Make thin stripes with the jam.

Senate Bean Soup

1 lb dried navy beans
8 cups hot water
¾ lb smoked ham hocks

1 small onion, chopped
1 T butter
salt and pepper to taste

1. Place beans into stock pot with hot water.
2. Add ham hocks and simmer, covered, 3 hours, stirring occasionally.
3. Remove ham hocks and allow to cool. Chop meat and return to soup.
4. Lightly brown the onion in butter. Add to soup.
5. Bring to a boil and season with salt and pepper.

Apple Pie

6 cups sliced apples
1 T lemon juice
½ cup sugar
½ cup packed brown sugar
2 T all-purpose flour
½ tsp cinnamon

¼ tsp nutmeg
double pie crust
2 T butter
1 egg yolk, beaten
2 tsp sugar
⅛ tsp cinnamon

1. Combine apples, lemon juice, sugars, flour, cinnamon, and nutmeg.
2. Spoon into bottom pie crust; dot with butter. Top with remaining crust. Cut slits in top crust. Brush with egg yolk. Mix sugar and cinnamon together and sprinkle over top.
3. Cover edges of crust loosely with thin strips of foil to prevent burning.
4. Bake at 450° for 15 minutes. Reduce heat to 350° and bake for an additional 50 minutes.

FOOD FACTS

- In countless surveys, apple pie has been chosen the favorite dessert in the United States.
- On 1800s farms, apple pie was a common breakfast food. It was considered a hearty way to start a hard day's work.
- Bean soup is on the menu in the Senate's restaurant every day.

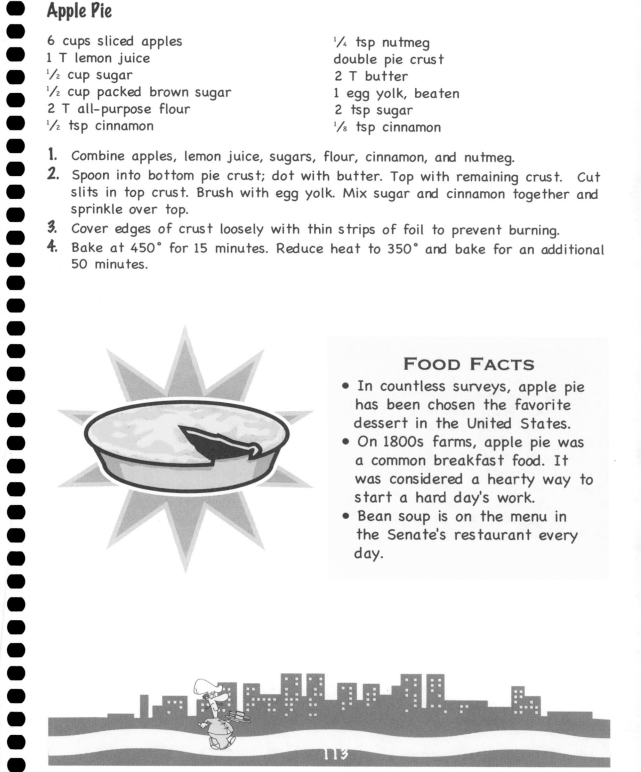

Eat Your Way Across the USA

Index

114

Other Fine Products Published by Geography Matters®

Cantering the Country (with CD-ROM)
Learning US geography is an adventure, especially when you can see how it ties in with so many other subjects. It's easy to see these connections when you use *Cantering the Country*. This 1–3 year unit study course will take you through each of the 50 states and the District of Columbia, teaching history, language arts, Bible, character, civics, and science along the way. Your first-sixth grade children can study all subjects except math and spelling in this course. Includes CD-ROM with over 150 activities and outline maps of each state. So saddle up your horses, strap on your thinking caps and get ready to explore America! 256 pages (with CD-ROM) - $39.95.

U.S. Activity Pages on CD-ROM
Here is the perfect addition to whatever U.S. geography curriculum you use. It is a CD-ROM filled with maps and activities. There are outline maps of each state and the nation, word scrambles, puzzles, mazes, words searches and more. Each activity is tied to a specific state and is a must for puzzle-loving kids. Some deal with the geographical features of the state while others give a fun and interesting look into the agriculture and industry of the area. This CD-ROM is included with the Cantering the Country course by Loreé Pettit & Dari Mullins, but we are making it available for separate purchase because it would fit in easily and be a great addition to any study on U.S. geography. $14.95

Galloping the Globe
Word searches, mazes, maps and more... clues, puzzles, and animals galore! What an enchanting way to learn geography—a unit study/discovery learning resource entitled *Galloping The Globe*. This geography based curriculum is geared towards the K–4th grade children and is a wonderful introduction to world geography using a notebooking approach to learning. It can be used from 1–3 years and covers all 7 continents. 240 pages - $24.95.

Trail Guide to Geography Series
The Trail Guide to Geography series uses an easy-to-follow format to teach essential geographical facts and features of our world. Written with the busy teacher in mind, each unique guide includes three different student levels and can be used for several years. There are a variety of ways to use the three-part manual. Teachers simply select which parts of the book will best meet their needs and objectives. Daily questions send students searching in an atlas, and yes... there are answers in the back of the book! Students complete assignments with outline maps, atlases, and other research materials. They learn capitals, place location, culture, climate, and much more!
Trail Guide to U.S. Geography - 128 pages - $18.95
Trail Guide to World Geography - 128 pages - $18.95
Trail Guide to Bible Geography - 128 pages - $18.95

USA/World Mark-It Map
Two-sided outline map with the world on one side and USA on the reverse. From youngsters learning continents and oceans to students depicting explorers routes, world wars, the 10/40 window, world missions, volcano ring of fire, world mineral deposits, and more. This map has an endless number of uses. Recommended for all grade levels. Write-on and wipe-off with Vis-a-Vis overhead projector pens (recommended). Laminated, 23˝ x 34˝ - $9.95.

Uncle Josh's Outline Map book or CD-ROM
Don't waste hours online searching for free outline maps only to be disappointed with their quality. Instead you can have these excellent outlines as handy as your bookshelf or computer. Make copies from the book format or print from your home computer. CD-ROM includes all 100+ maps from the book PLUS an additional 23 new maps. New maps include: maps of each Canadian territory and province, physical relief maps of each continent, and physical relief of Afghanistan and Pakistan. You've got the whole world covered in this one-of-a-kind set of outline maps! 112 pages - $19.95 or CD-ROM - $26.95.

Continents Map Set
If you enjoy using outline maps but wish they were larger, at 17˝ x 22˝+, these are it! Great for use with any high school curriculum or for many varieties of detailed drawing and labeling map projects. Eight maps include: North America, South America, Africa, Europe, Asia (23˝ x 34˝), Australia with Pacific Ocean islands (23˝ x 34˝) with inset of Antarctica, plus BONUS USA map. A perfect companion to the "Conquering the Continents" study in the *Ultimate Geography and Timeline Guide!* $12.95 paper - $24.95 laminated.

Bible Land Activity Map Set
Studying Bible history or Ancient Civilizations? Need more detailed maps of the area known as the Cradle of Civilization or of the Europe and Middle East region? These 17˝ x 22˝ outline maps provide numerous opportunities for your students to depict their history studies on a map. Set includes Europe and the Middle East, Ancient Civilizations, and two double-sided Israel/Eastern Mediterranean maps along with a BONUS 23˝ x 34˝ Mark-It Timeline of History. $12.95 paper - $24.95 laminated.

Mark-It Timeline of History
Record historical data as you learn for great hands-on learning with this activity timeline poster. Dated from 4000 BC to 2050 AD on the front. The back is ready to write in your own dates for in-depth studies. Laminated for durability and write-on wipe-off qualities. 23˝ x 34˝ - $9.95 laminated.

Timeline Figures CD-ROMs
Now our Bible and historical timeline figures are available in color on CD-ROM! Print as many as you need when you need them. These figures are appealing in art style, simple to understand, and greatly increase understanding of the flow of historical events. Color coding and icons help students remember their facts and add interest to any timeline.
Historical Timeline Figures CD-ROM - $24.95
Bible Timeline Figures CD-ROM - $24.95

Contact us for our current catalog, or log on to www.geomatters.com. Wholesale accounts welcome.

(800) 426-4650 – www.geomatters.com